Dale Sm

Air-Sea Rescue

in World War Two

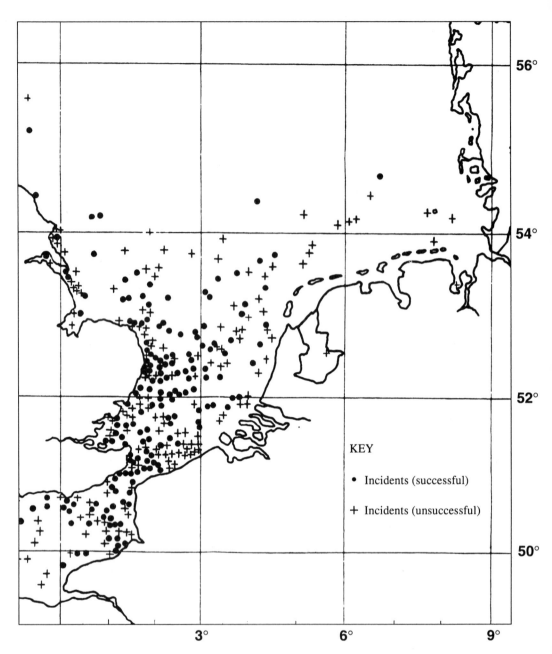

Air-Sea Rescue incidents of all kinds April to September 1944 (Overlord & Market Garden Operations excepted)
(PRO, AIR 20/1283 © Crown Copyright. Reproduced with the permission of the Controller of Her Majesty's Stationery Office.)

Air-Sea Rescue

in World War Two

A first-hand account of the Royal Navy North
Sea Rescue Motor Launches

ALAN ROWE

WITH THE COLLABORATION OF ANDY ANDREWS

ALAN SUTTON PUBLISHING LIMITED

First published in the United Kingdom in 1995 by
Alan Sutton Publishing Limited
Phoenix Mill · Far Thrupp · Stroud · Gloucestershire

British Library Cataloguing in Publication Data

A catalogue record for this book is available from the British Library

ISBN 0-7509-0911-0

Jacket illustration: Glider, with crew in dinghy, September, 1944
Inset: 69th Flotilla in line ahead

Typeset in 10/12 Times.
Typesetting and origination by
Alan Sutton Publishing Limited.
Printed in Great Britain by
The Alden Press Ltd., Oxford and Northampton.

Contents

Illustrations

Introduction

The cold and stormy waters of the North Sea were the final enemy to be overcome by brave men struggling to bring back their damaged aircraft, after hitting at the heart of Germany. This book records their heroism, not only in pressing home the attack on their target, but also in defying the hazards of ditching and surviving, sometimes for days, in a hostile sea. It tells, too, of the patience and endurance of those who sought and rescued them, often in gales which kept other vessels in harbour and grounded the search aircraft. This was a little-known branch of the Navy's famous Coastal Forces.

The Air-Sea Rescue service in general made a vital contribution to the morale of the RAF and to the success of the war effort during the long years when the offensive against the German Reich and its industrial base could be maintained only by bombing raids across the wide expanse of the North Sea. It was equally important later, during the course of the advance across the low countries, when the safety of fighter pilots was a top priority, and the USAAF was sending massive numbers of aircraft on daylight sorties against industrial targets.

It is almost always assumed that the rescue service was provided entirely by the High Speed Launches of the RAF. The Royal Navy, however, had its own Rescue Motor Launches, based in units of four boats in harbours all around the coast of the British Isles, in such places as Appledore in Devon, Falmouth, Newhaven, Yarmouth, Lowestoft, Immingham on the Humber, and as far North as Stornaway. These boats formed a branch of its Coastal Forces and were adapted versions of the Fairmile 'B'-type ML, which was used in large numbers for convoy protection and also to provide support for raids such as those on St Nazaire and on islands in the Mediterranean.

Although they were much slower, they had the advantage of being larger, with more accommodation, and capable of remaining at sea for longer periods. With a conventional hull, they were able to be used in any weather and at any distance from land, whereas high speed craft, like the HSLs and the Navy's MTBs, were of little use in rough seas. They deserve honourable mention in the record of the Navy's wartime activities.

This book gives a true personal account of the many rescues and other operations carried out by the 69th RML Flotilla in the North Sea from 1943 to 1945. It is based on the log of the flotilla leader, HMRML 547, on signals and reports preserved by its Senior Officer, Lieut. T.D. Andrews RNVR and the recollections of members of the crews. He and the author have carried out extensive research in order to discover the stories behind the rescues, linking the experiences of the airmen concerned to those of the rescuers. Thanks in this respect are due to the RAF Museum at Hendon, Mr H.T.N. Ling of the Bomber Command Association, The Coastal Forces Veterans' Association, The Public Record Office at Kew, and The RN and RAF Historical Sections of the Ministry of Defence. The Research Division of the HQ USAF Historical Research Centre at the Maxwell Air Force base has provided much very useful information. The observations made by glider crews passing overhead in Chapter 16 are reported in Cornelius Ryan's *A Bridge Too Far*. Other books and authors consulted are acknowledged in the text. Our thanks also to Roger Freeman, Martin Middlebrook, William Dolan, Hugh Melville and Derek (Spike) Gill.

The book also illustrates, in an informal way, the story of the development of the ASR service during the course of the war from extremely modest beginnings. At the start, it consisted of little more than a random collection of small yachts and motor boats, based in various harbours, with no co-ordination, training or equipment of any kind. Lieut. Andrews, in fact, was put in charge of one of these, when he was a completely untrained Petty Officer in 1940, so that he was well aware of the progress made during the next five years.

Even though things are so very different today, with rescue helicopters and satellite navigational aids, which can pinpoint a small boat in distress and remove the guesswork involved in dead reckoning, there are some lessons to be learnt from past experience. There have been recent cases where air and sea searches have failed because the boats or dinghies concerned were ill-equipped and the searchers lacked experience of the effects of wind and tide on the movement of both boats and aircraft. There was, for example, the case of the motor-boat which was carried from the Welsh coast to Lundy Island without being spotted. One of its occupants survived only because it drifted near enough for him to swim ashore. The search had been unsuccessful because insufficient allowance had been made for the power of the wind. This book could be of some benefit, therefore, even to today's high-powered technicians, whose technology still needs at times a human touch.

Public Record Office documents consulted:
AIR 14/391, 779, 2791, 3213–3227, 3410, 3466–3470, 3473, 3481, 3482–3483
AIR 15/595–599, 676, 4147, 5393, 5426, 5429, 5472, 5556, 5606, 5620, 5621, 5650, 5709
AIR 20/214, 1283, 4318–20, 4567, 4703–10, 6193–6207
AIR 27/100, 258, 651, 687, 796, 802, 1234, 1351, 1406, 1497, 1657, 1822, 1908, 2090
AIR 29/443, 444, 449
AIR 50/189

CHAPTER 1

Wearie Willie

As we came out of the large Nissen hut which served as the base cinema, the warm summer evening was humming with the steady drone of aero-engines. There was still enough light in the sky to look up and see the dark shapes of scores of Avro-Lancasters, circling at various heights above Hull and the entrance to the Humber, like a swarm of huge and deadly bees.

'No sleep for us tonight,' said Mac.

'No,' I agreed. 'I'd rather be at sea, though, than sticking my neck out up there.'

We came out of the gate at the entrance to Flag Officer Humber's headquarters on to the rough road which bordered the river. Across the dirty brown waters of the Humber, the shaded lamps of the Hull waterfront showed up dimly in the fast-fading light. Nearer to us, we could see the riding lights of ships at anchor, waiting to enter Immingham Dock, where we now identified ourselves to the policeman on duty and then made our way across the lock gates towards the basin where our ships were berthed.

The noise of aircraft was fading as the bomber stream reached its ceiling, formed up and headed eastwards into the night.

'I pity the poor bastards who get that lot dropped on them tonight,' said Mac.

'And the blokes who get the chop,' I added. 'Let's hope that if any ditch in the drink we can get to them. I'm fed up with tearing around the ocean day after day and never finding anything.'

'Mac' MacLaren and I were sub lieutenants in the 'Wavy Navy', otherwise known as the RNVR, with the imposing title of First Lieutenant of each of two RMLs of the Navy's Coastal Forces, based at Immingham. We were each second in command of a somewhat unusual type of boat, which was a Fairmile 'B' type Motor Launch adapted and specially equipped for Air-Sea Rescue. Most people thought that only the High Speed Launches, or HSLs, of the RAF carried out this task, but the Navy supplied larger, more seaworthy, though slower Rescue Motor Launches to do the long distance, rough weather work. These were indispensible in the wide and stormy northern part of the sea, for HSLs, like the Navy's MTBs, were fine for speeding over the surface of a calm sea, but as soon as it got a bit choppy they had had it. We, on the other hand, were often heading out to sea in a raging gale, when most other craft were kept safe in harbour. As we lived on board, we could stay at sea for several days.

It was late July, 1943, a turning point in the war, when Britain was sending increasing numbers of Lancs and Halifaxes across the North Sea, night after night, carrying massive bomb-loads into the heart of Germany. The Americans, too, had begun to join in, making the first mass daylight raids, although they were to find them more expensive than they had anticipated at first. It gave a certain grim satisfaction to those of us who had been through the blitzes in London, Plymouth and Bristol to see the tables turned in this way, although no one could feel anything but horror at the heavy casualties on both sides. A hundred of our bombers or more could be lost in a single raid, and the German dead could be counted in thousands, although we were not aware of this at the time.

Mac and I clambered down the dockside ladder and made our way along the catamarans floating between the boats moored bows-on to the bank. On our left, the number 547, in large figures on the bow, indicated my ship and on the right lay Mac's ship, number 550.

'Coming aboard for a tot, Alan?' asked MacLaren, who was a tough but cheery Scotsman, older and with longer experience in Coastal Forces than I.

'No thanks,' I replied, 'I'd better get changed and ready for sea.'

'Jimmy's back,' I heard Boswell, the AB on watch, call down the forward hatch as I climbed the 'mediterranean' ladder attached to the ship's side and reached our quarter deck.

'Cup of char, sir?' he asked, coming aft to greet me. 'Captain's gone to ops for orders.'

(Jimmy, or Jimmy the One, was the universal Navy name for a First Lieutenant. On small ships he was responsible for just about every aspect of the ship's routine: guns, ammunition supplies, charts, signals, navigation, general maintenance, discipline, cleanliness, food, bonded stores, tobacco and rum issue, keeping the log and generally carrying the can for anything that went wrong!)

'Not yet,' I replied. 'Tell the Coxswain to clear decks, ready for sea. We'll have hot drinks on the way out,' and I hurried down the companion to our neat little wardroom, with its mahogany bunks on each side, fitted cupboards and coal-fired stove. I changed from my shore-going uniform into old trousers, sea-boots, thick white submariner's jersey and duffle coat and made my way to the wheelhouse to prepare my charts and look up the code letters and the Very's flare signals for the night, which would identify friend and foe.

By the time Andy, or to be more precise Lieutenant Andrews, our skipper, returned with sailing orders, we were ready for sea, the galley fire was stoked, the kettle was on, potatoes were baking in the oven and my North Sea charts were laid out on the chart table in the wheelhouse, together with my navigator's note-book and chronometer. Soon the twin Hall-

547 approaching dinghy. Note sick bay aft of funnel and boom out amidships.

Scott petrol engines were started up and, together with 550, we eased our way out of our mooring and entered the lock which would give us entry to the river. Within minutes the ebbing tide was carrying us away from *HMS Beaver II*, the headquarters of C-in-C Humber, past Hull on the opposite bank, past Grimsby and Cleethorpes, to the gate in the boom which protected the river mouth.

People on shore, used to the black-out, would have thought it strange to see so many lights shining over the inky sea: the gate vessel showed the all-clear for exit, buoys winked their various identities to show us the swept channels, and on the horizon the powerful beam from the Humber Light Vessel beckoned us out to the open sea. Andy was the Senior Officer of our four-boat flotilla, which meant that we were always the leading boat, throwing the main responsibility for the navigation on me. So, with 550 following our stern light, we headed due East, past the light vessel and out into the dark, empty sea beyond the coastal convoy route, where we were normally the only ships to be seen.

Andy, in his early thirties, had been a keen amateur sailor before the war, with a small boat of his own, which he moored in the Thames estuary. He had come to Immingham from Harbour Defence Motor Launches based at Plymouth only about eight weeks before. I had joined 547, fresh from my Coastal Forces training course, at Fort William in Scotland, not long before him, so we were still, to some extent, gaining experience in the special skills needed for rescue work in the treacherous conditions of the northern sea.

Our task was, as usual, to make our way to a patrol position about 50 miles east of the Humber, cut engines and wait for orders. At an economical speed of 12 knots, we should arrive there at about three in the morning. Meanwhile, in the big underground ops room at Nore Headquarters, near London, the ASR section would be filtering the information coming through from ships and aircraft and preparing to direct patrol vessels to positions where lights had been seen or from which damaged aircraft had sent out mayday calls for help.

Our course took us through a gap in the East coast minefield, although we didn't usually worry much whether we were in the minefield or not, relying on our fairly shallow draught to see us through. What we needed to look out for was the occasional mine which had broken adrift from its moorings and lay floating on the surface. These we despatched with fire from the Lewis guns on our bridge or the Oerlikon cannon aft.

On the bridge, Andy, the Coxswain and the watch on deck kept a look out for any mines or other strange objects, whilst I, leaning over my table, laid out the course on the chart by the process known as dead reckoning. As this was a routine operation, the navigation was simple. We had no log to measure our speed through the water, but we could make a good estimate by relating it to the engine revs. We had drawn up a scale showing how speed corresponded to engine revs in different weather conditions by timing the distance between fixed points such as buoys or landmarks. Having recorded revs and speed, all one had to take into consideration was the state of the tide and the currents, using information marked on the chart. Things could get a lot more complicated, at times, when rapid changes of course and speed had to be logged and marked on the chart, or allowance made for rough weather and strong winds. As enemy E-Boats usually kept nearer to the convoy routes, however, and the wind this evening was light, there was not much to worry about.

Except, that is, for poor Jack Reeson, Ordinary Seaman. When I left the wheelhouse, to go into the open for a breath of air, Tom Goodwin, a strapping country lad from Gloucestershire pointed to a figure lying prone on the deck beside the bridge. Merely leaving the shelter of the river was enough to prostrate the cockney boy. He would eat nothing and move only with extreme difficulty from now until we were back in sight of land again, when he would become his usual cheery, willing self. Whether he was also a highly skilled con man we never discovered: moves were already afoot to have him put ashore for good. I was to run

Lieut. T.D. Andrews

into him long after, sweeping up the leaves in the grounds of Greenwich Naval College. There were no flies on Jack, it seemed! There he was, in a comfortable berth, close to home and to his beloved Dot, who was the focus of his entire existence.

On the other hand, if his disability was not genuine, how could he have resisted the thick, sweet, comforting cocoa and hand-warming baked potatoes which our chef, Arthur Greenwood, now brought up from his cramped, coal-fired galley. Arthur was so small and so pale and thin that he seemed unlikely to survive the heat and the confined and often chaotic conditions in which he strove to keep us fed. Stoking the fire and juggling with pots and pans as the boat corkscrewed and plunged in a North Sea gale must have been one of the least enviable jobs in Coastal Forces. I used to wonder whether he managed to eat anything himself after he had finished preparing our meals in those conditions. Now, however, as he lingered to get a breath of fresh air, he had his usual quiet smile under his curly brown hair, and seemed quite contented with his lot.

With the course and time of arrival at our waiting position set, I was soon able to retire aft and turn in for a while in my bunk in our small wardroom. Lulled by the hum of the engines and the movement of the boat over the gentle swell, I drifted off to sleep, to be re-awakened by the silence and the change in movement as the engines were stopped and the waves began to roll us gently from side to side. It was time to take over the watch and jam myself into the starboard corner of the bridge, half seated on the signal locker, where the flags were kept,

Lieut. Andrews and part of crew. Left to right: (Back row) Reeson, Gower (cox), Andy, Speed, Greenwood. (Front row) Wilson, Cannon

while Andy took advantage of the lull in activities. Only when things were quiet could we divide the watchkeeping. When we were busy with a search we might both be on duty for as much as thirty-six hours continuously.

Would this, I wondered, be another of those occasions when we waited patiently, sometimes in intense discomfort, well into the next day before the recall signal brought us back to base, with nothing to show for our efforts? That had, so far, been our usual experience, and Andy and I were beginning to feel frustrated by the lack of communication with other parts of the ASR set-up and the apparent inadequacy of the service.

'What's the buzz then?' asked Flash Speed, one of our stokers and our Mr Fix-it, as he climbed out of the engine-room hatch to seize the chance of a smoke and a chat. 'Ain't we going home yet? I've got a nice little bit of stuff lined up for tonight. What's the betting we'll be back by four?'

'You'll be lucky,' said Tom, 'All that lot was heading North-East, and they'll be coming back our way. Anyway, your first stop'll have to be the Naafi to get some decent grub. I'm fed up with soya sausage and tinned greengages.'

Flash was our mess caterer, with a cockney's talent for doing a crafty fiddle and making a bob or two on the side. The sausages and greengages were the free extras which we received as what were called 'comforts', to compensate for the conditions in which we had to live at sea, and he used them skilfully, in fact, to supplement the Navy's messing allowance and to help provide, at minimum cost, a high standard of living through his contacts on shore.

Suddenly, the hum of our wireless transmitter starting up silenced the conversation. Jim

Cannon, our leading telegraphist, down below in his cabin, was acknowledging a message from Nore.

'That's it then. Steak and chips tonight lads and a run ashore,' said Flash, cheerily.

The message handed up to me from the radio cabin soon dashed his hopes.

'Get below and start up the engines,' I ordered. 'Goodwin, go and give the captain a shake. Tell him we're ordered to head East.'

The orders were, in fact to go to our outer patrol position, 50 miles further eastwards, plumb in the middle of the North Sea. What this meant it was difficult to fathom, except that there was not much prospect of spending the evening ashore. With a gentle sea, and a bright dawn gradually spreading across the sky ahead of us, we were at least able to savour the special pleasure that the seaman's life can give, even in wartime. In what resembled, except for its camouflage paint, its yellow air-sea-rescue decks and its weaponry, an outsize millionaire's yacht, we often felt, on a peaceful, sunny day, as if we were on a luxury cruise, until the radio called us back to reality.

On position and stopped again, we were able to relax and enjoy the fresh air and sunshine, whilst the duty watch kept a lookout for stray aircraft. It was Sunday morning, so calm, so peaceful, that war seemed far away, and it was difficult to remind ourselves that somewhere over there to the East of us they were clearing up the night's destruction.

'Sorry lads, it's corned dog from now on,' apologised Flash at lunchtime, as large thick corned beef sandwiches were handed around to the watchkeepers on the bridge. But food was almost immediately forgotten as Jock Wilson, the port after lookout, suddenly cried: 'Aircraft, red one hundred!'

To our amazement, out of the thin, hazy cloud which hung like a wispy curtain to the south-west, there emerged squadron after squadron of long, silver shapes, gleaming brightly as they caught the rays of the sun. They glided overhead in perfect formation, a vast aerial armada, several squadrons wide and high, filling the sky above us. We had seen the occasional B-17 Flying Fortress on training flights, but this was the first time we had seen them gathered in such force, obviously about to make a mass daylight raid on Germany. So this was why we were being kept here. A big operation was taking place.

'Where d'ye think they're heading for, sir?' asked Wilson, a dark-haired young Scotsman.

'Well, if they stay on a nor'easterly course, it could be Kiel, perhaps,' I replied.

'Lancs last night and Fortresses today – round the clock bombing! That should speed up the end of the war!' said Gower, the Coxswain.

'It won't speed up the recall, though,' Flash reflected glumly. 'We'll have to wait now until they all get back safe, and I wouldn't give much odds on that, not flying over Germany in broad daylight.'

Certainly, even if none of the Lancs had ditched – and that was beginning to seem more likely, the longer we waited – we would still be staying here for a good while yet. And quite probably we might at last have the opportunity to justify our existence with a rescue. In fact, however, hours later, as the long summer evening was beginning to fade into night, the surprising order came that we were to return to base and refuel ready for sea again.

In the two months since Andy and I had been together on HMRML 547, as she was officially called, this kind of disappointment had occurred repeatedly. Hours of waiting on our patrol position in all kinds of weather had resulted in just a few orders to head for a suspected dinghy. But each time we had been recalled after a fruitless search and, to add to our frustration, whenever we had seen a search aircraft it had been impossible to contact it by radio to find out if it had found anything. Both boats and aircraft were supposed to keep watch on the 500kcs international distress frequency, and if an aircraft found a dinghy, it was supposed to send out a signal on which we could home with our direction-finding equipment,

Sub Lieut. Rowe and part of crew. Left to right: (Back row) Boswell, Alan, Goodwin, (Temp). (Front row) Williams, (Previous M.M.), Bowler.

but at that time the organisation was so poor that communication seemed impossible. When, we wondered, were we going to be allowed to do our job effectively. We didn't want any of our bombers to be forced to ditch in the sea, of course, but obviously they didn't all get home safely and there could be chaps out there waiting in vain for rescue, while we were prevented from finding them by what seemed to be an inefficient organisation.

Next day found us waiting impatiently for orders, and sharing, over a lunch-time gin with MacLaren and his skipper, 'Shep' Sheppard, our moans at the lack of information and positive action. It was not until the following day that we were both heading out of the Humber again, this time with orders to sail north, up the swept channel, to a waiting position far to the east of Scarborough. What were they playing at now?

I had just gone down aft to the wardroom to taste once again the familiar delights of stewed soya sausages and tinned greengages, when the signal reached Andy on the bridge. An actual dinghy, with three men in it, had been reported in a position just south-east of the Dogger Bank, so I plotted a course, allowing for the tide and currents in the area and resumed my interrupted meal. Back in the wheelhouse as the afternoon wore on, I waited to adjust the chart to any changes of course which might be necessary, but, although we saw a search aircraft, it seemed intent on ignoring us. No one was transmitting on the rescue frequency, the aircraft made no attempt to lead us on a different course, so we kept plodding on and keeping a sharp lookout, with 550 at visibility distance to starboard, to cover as wide a stretch of sea as possible. Up in the crow's nest, Clem Woodhead, the father of the crew, was getting tired and stiff as his watch went slowly by. Clem was the object of special respect from the younger lads, having been full back for Hull City before the war. Now, suddenly, he sprang into life again.

'Halifax red one zero. Seems to be circling, sir.'

Yes, indeed, the aircraft was swinging around in tight circles and there, beneath it, the white triangle of a sail was clearly visible on the calm sea. Now, of course, it was full speed ahead, racing with 550 in the direction of the sail – although obviously this was not a dinghy. As we drew near, it turned out to be a fishing vessel, with a crowd of cheering Americans lining the side to greet us.

We pulled alongside to discover that the vessel was a 40ft Danish boat from Fredrikshavn named the *Ternan*, skippered by a bearded elderly man, with a boy as the only crew. On the deck lay a tarpaulin with a large 'SOS' painted on it, which the RAF search plane had spotted some time earlier. At the Americans' request, we gave the Dane some cartons of duty-free cigarettes and we received in return some very welcome fresh fish, straight off the Dogger Bank. In fact, through not being fished in war-time, the Dogger was swarming with fish, and as I looked down into the sheltered, clear water between the two boats, I could see shoals of them swimming between the keels. We tried to persuade the fishermen to come back to England with us, but they refused, fearing reprisals against their family if they did so. At length, sharing our ten airmen with 550, which lay on the other side of the fishing-boat, we cast off and watched them head for home. What sort of reception, we wondered, would they get from the Germans, who must surely guess what had happened, especially if they found English cigarettes on board.

'Doc' Bowler, our Jeordie Sick Bay Attendant, dressed the slight wounds that some of our guests had sustained and they were settled comfortably in the sick bay and wardroom, with a bottle of Scotch to put some life back into them, although this was hardly necessary. They were delighted to be safely in the hands of the Navy and keen to tell us of their adventures.

We discovered that they had been the lead plane in one of the lower groups of Fortresses which we had seen on the previous Sunday. *Wearie Willie*, as it was called, was a B-17 of 544th Bomb Squadron, 384th Bomb Group, heading for Hamburg, which had already been badly hit by the Lancasters the night before. They passed through the heavy flak without damage and dropped their bombs on the target, largely obscured by the smoke from fires started in the previous raid, but then found themselves in serious trouble. The Germans had called up all available aircraft, including even twin-engined night-fighters from Holland, to concentrate an attack on them as they withdrew towards the coast. The enemy came in to the attack head-on, so that *Wearie Willie*, at the head of its group, was in the most dangerous position of all. One after another six of the eight aircraft in the low group were hit and fell away from the main formation, to be pounced on and shot down by the surrounding fighters. But *Wearie Willie's* pilot, Lieutenant Estes, sticking to his orders, continued to 'fly as briefed', refusing to leave the one other remaining plane and seek shelter with the main formation above him.

'Watch out for those fighters, I'm out of ammunition,' called Sergeant Ursta, the ball-turret gunner.

'Just stay there,' replied Estes calmly, 'and pretend you're firing.'

Sgt McDuffie, the tail gunner, had spent all his ammunition, too, and he also kept on tracking his guns to scare off the fighters. In the waist Sergeants Self and O'Donnell managed to keep on firing although, as the fighters relentlessly followed the aircraft out to sea, *Wearie Willie* suffered more and more damage. The oxygen supply of the top turret was knocked out, the left wing-tip was shattered, three engines were hit and 20mm cannon shells began exploding in the nose. The explosions knocked the bombardier, 2nd Lieutenant Davis, and the navigator, 2nd Lieutenant Dubois, back into the tunnel, ripping off their helmets and oxygen masks. But, disregarding the now gaping hole in the nose, the two men, both without oxygen, forced their way back to their guns, charged them and continued to fire.

'What do you recommend in this situation?' Davis coolly asked his pilot.

'I recommend ditching,' answered Estes unconcernedly, laughing as he spoke. 'Pass the order to prepare to ditch.'

Ursta, hearing 'one hell of an explosion' and seeing the engines disintegrating, called to his captain, 'Say, don't you think it's a good idea to get out of here?'

'Sure,' was Estes' brief reply. But, before Ursta could put on his parachute, Sergeant Cochran, the engineer, had reached him with the order to prepare for ditching.

As the stricken plane fell out of formation, in a shallow dive towards the sea, three fighters followed her down, continuing to attack. Suddenly, seeing a Focke-Wulf 190 coming straight for the nose, Estes flung the aircraft into a steep dive down to 5,000 feet. Davis, caught off balance, was thrown through the top hatch and the other members of the crew were unable to catch him, but he managed to grasp the fuselage. When the plane levelled off again, it threw him back into the radio room, where he was joined by the other crew members, as Sergeant Wagner continued to transmit a mayday signal.

When *Wearie Willie* was too low for frontal attacks, the fighters swooped in from astern and they were still attacking as the aircraft hit the water. Shells were exploding in the plane and in the water around. Then, to everyone's great relief, presumably because they were short of fuel, the enemy left.

After the ditching, the crew had time only to scramble into their two life-rafts and paddle about 50 feet before the Fortress took its last weary plunge. Then someone thought to compliment the pilot on the beautiful landing.

'I didn't do it,' said Estes. 'I levelled off about 20 feet above the water and told the Good Lord He had control, and the Good Lord sure made a wonderful landing.'

One raft had been punctured by flak and required considerable patching, pumping and baling to keep it afloat. As the ten men bobbed about in the rafts, about 60 miles from the enemy coast, time seemed to pass slowly, but they were still able to joke about their predicament. They divided out their rations, so as to make them last ten days.

'Say, is this all the food we're going to get?' the engineer, Sergeant Cochran, complained. 'Don't we get any fresh meat?'

'Not unless we draw lots to see who we're going to kill,' said Sergeant Burton, one of the gunners.

'I guess we ought to eat Fred Wagner first,' O'Donnell suggested, 'he's nice and chunky.'

'Let's kill him right now,' joked Ursa, 'before he loses weight!'

For a full 38 hours they sat in the cramped, wet and uncomfortable dinghies: two weary nights of tedious pitching and baling. Then they saw in the distance what appeared to be the sail of a small boat. Seeing it come nearer, they paddled slowly in its direction. About three hours later, they were close enough to shout to the skipper. They saw him let loose a buoy and put his flag out and then come towards them. After he had picked them up, the Danish fisherman explained that he thought at first they were Germans and he had hesitated to come to them sooner. When he heard their shouts, he realised they were either English or American.

The problem now was, were they going to allow the Dane to take them back to harbour to be made prisoners, or could they persuade him to sail with them to England? The bombardier, Lieutenant Davis, described to us how they told their rescuer that they would rather go back to the dinghies than allow themselves to become prisoners of the Germans. The skipper, on the other hand, was afraid of the harm that would come to his wife and family if he helped the Americans to escape. In the end, he was persuaded to go westwards as far as his fuel would allow, provided he had enough left to get back to port. When he reached the Dogger Bank, he stopped. Luckily, the following morning they sighted the Handley Page Halifax, which circled them for several hours. They took a tarpaulin and painted, in white letters, 'SOS BRING BOAT', and the Halifax replied with a signal from its Aldis lamp, 'Rescue launch coming'. Some hours later we arrived.

At last we enjoyed the sweet taste of success. Co-operation with the RAF had not been perfect, but we had ten American airmen safe on board. However, these weren't the three men in a dinghy whom we had been sent to look for.

'Our new course is 058 degrees,' I called up to Andy, having adjusted my chart.

'Aren't we taking them back, sir?' asked the coxswain, Gower, an experienced Leading Seaman who always took over the wheel for special manoeuvres. He had previously been coxswain to 'Harpie' Lloyd, a noted MTB skipper.

'We still have a search on,' said Andy. 'There's a dinghy somewhere ahead, don't forget.'

Dusk was approaching as we reached the original position for which we had been heading, but for as long as there was light enough we carried out a square search. This meant that the two boats, at visibility distance from each other, started from the given position to search an expanding area of sea by going increasing distances North, West, South, East and then North again. Without the help of search aircraft, this was a slow and unrewarding process, for a dinghy was a small and difficult object to spot at sea level. Britain during the war kept double summer time, which meant that on a fine summer's evening darkness was not complete until midnight. We then had to stop our search, cut engines and wait for daylight, keeping a sharp lookout, for there could be enemy boats and planes nearer to us than our own.

Andy and I took turns to snatch a few hours' sleep before dawn brought light enough to resume our search. Then off we went again, round and round, in ever-increasing squares, getting more and more frustrated by the absence of search aircraft. About mid-day, Walsh, the assistant telegraphist, handed up another signal ordering us to yet another position further West.

'Well, that was a pretty useless waste of time,' Andy commented, whilst I resignedly adjusted my chart and gave him a fresh course to steer.

Hardly had we started to head for the new position, when Walsh picked up a call from an aircraft which directed us to turn back eastwards again to a position quite close to the Danish coast. We had hardly adjusted to this before a message from base told us to ignore the aircraft's instructions and return to Immingham. So after chasing to and fro over countless miles of empty sea, we finally found ourselves landing our American friends at midnight and refuelling ready for sea once more.

'Well,' said Mac, as we toasted our first success with a quick glass of Scotch, before getting some well-earned rest, 'we've something to celebrate at last.'

'But it was pure chance, no thanks to the people on shore,' I said. 'We have no idea what became of the other dinghies we were supposed to be chasing.'

'We'll have a report worth reading this time,' commented Andy. 'Perhaps it will make them pull their fingers out and see that we get better communication with search aircraft. Why wasn't that Lanc. able to call us up when it sighted us?'

These were questions which Andy set about solving in the weeks that followed, making reports and suggestions which were gradually to help us to become much more efficient by establishing procedures for co-operating with aircraft. But meanwhile there was much more work to keep us busy.

What we were to discover much later was that we were involved in a massive onslaught on the city of Hamburg. The first British raid, on July 24th, produced few casualties amongst our bombers because, for the first time, a new device called 'window' was used. Thousands

Normal 'B' type ML

of strips of aluminium foil were poured from our aircraft, forming a curtain which threw the enemy radar defences into confusion and prevented them from directing the night-fighters on to suitable targets. This was followed immediately by the daylight raid. And while we were bringing our Americans back, a series of further heavy raids had produced a fire-storm in which massive destruction had been wrought and tens of thousands had died. Bomber Harris had called this 'Operation Gomorrah', a title which did in fact describe the horror of that week. Ironically, however, this was the most anti-Nazi city in Germany, and many of those who died in the raids were active opponents of the régime. Hiltgunt Zassenhaus in her fascinating book, *Walls*, about the anti-Nazi resistance in Hamburg, describes how her family's house was destroyed and their work for the resistance was hampered as a result of the bombing. One casualty, for example, was a man who used his office in the docks to help dissidents escape on ships going to Sweden. Another victim was an old lady, who actually had a son in America. On her mantelpiece she kept a postcard from him, bearing a picture of the Statue of Liberty. She was killed by an American bomb.

I have discovered since that our Americans were to go back to duty and survive the war. Only the plump Sergeant Wagner was due to undergo another unpleasant, though remarkably lucky experience. On January 4th, 1944, Lieutenant Estes and his crew took part in a raid on Kiel. As they left the target, they found that some of the bombs had stuck. Sgt Wagner went into the bomb bay to release them, but lost consciousness when his oxygen failed, causing him to slip out of the plane. His comrades thought he had been killed but, in actual fact, he revived at a lower altitude and was able to let out his parachute in time to land and be taken prisoner.

On the day following the rescue, it was our turn to have a day off duty, but very soon the increasing weight of the air offensive was to take us back into the eastern part of the North Sea for another very different type of rescue, which might easily have resulted in our needing to be rescued ourselves.

Let me first, however, retrace the events which had led up to our being appointed to this branch of Coastal Forces.

CHAPTER 2

How it all Began

'You've seen a bit of action, then,' said the grizzled old admiral, examining my papers.

'Yes, sir,' I replied, trying to look alert and keen, since this was my final interview before being granted a commission in the RNVR.

'You'd like to see some more, wouldn't you?'

'Er – yes, sir.' There was no other possible answer, if that brand new officer's uniform, with its wavy gold ring, was not to be left unclaimed at Austin Reed's Brighton branch.

'Plenty of action in Coastal Forces. That's the branch for you, don't you think?'

'Er – yes, sir,' I responded, weakly. The challenge could not be refused.

So that was it. End of interview. I had volunteered for Coastal Forces. I hadn't meant to, of course. We had all been given the opportunity to state our preferences and I had asked if I might be found a job as a liaison officer with the Free French, on a destroyer perhaps, since I hoped to return to London University after the war and complete a French Honours degree. I reckoned that would keep my French up to scratch and even make me pretty well bilingual by the time the war was over.

Now I felt a bit like the matelot in the old naval joke, who went to Heaven and, wherever he stood at Archangel's morning divisions, always managed to get put in the Harping Party for the day – a cold damp job, sitting on a cloud and twanging a harp for hours on end. He tells his mate:

'The day before, see, I got caught 'cos I was on the left of the line. So this time I falls in on the right. And the Chief PO angel goes: "Heavenly sweepers, Archangels' sweepers, Heavenly Gate chipping party, Cherubs' wings oiling party, Harping party" – and there was I in the Harping party again. I wasn't half chokka!'

There was I in Coastal Forces, with no way out. If you passed out high enough on the class list, which I had done, you were supposed to have priority in your choice of where you would like to serve. There was indeed a liaison job going, but that went to another chap, low down on the pass list, who had no knowledge whatever of French. Typical, I thought!

There was a great recruiting drive on at that time – the end of 1942 – for Coastal Forces. A number of our entry found themselves similarly heading that way. It was about the only branch of the Navy having much success or attracting favourable attention through its daring exploits in the Channel and on the East Coast. We had had a visit and a pep talk from the famous Robert Hichens, from *HMS Beehive*, at Felixstowe, encouraging us to seek adventure on the little ships, the MTBs and MGBs which attacked German coastal convoys and protected our own from the E-boats. He was unfortunately to die not long afterwards in a battle with the enemy. In fact, casualties in those frail little craft were quite heavy and replacements were regularly needed, which was another reason for our being press-ganged into that service.

So now, having exchanged my bell-bottoms for my smart new Sub Lieutenant's uniform, I embarked on a series of courses which would prepare me for becoming a hero – preferably not a dead one, although the odds were not too favourable!

It was true, I had seen some quite fierce action in the previous six months. Coming from Plymouth I had also known what it was to be a civilian in a front line town, with frequent air raids and news of naval catastrophes from the very beginning of the war. In the first air raids, the menacing drone of enemy planes, the crack of ack-ack fire and the scream of falling bombs had struck terror into people's hearts, but gradually we had grown accustomed to the noise and the heightened tension and realised it was more important to get some sleep than to leap out of bed whenever the siren sounded. We had acquired a fatalistic disregard for danger, except when it grew really close. So at least I was able to accept the situation philosophically. There was danger wherever you went, but plenty of fun too, and I had always enjoyed messing about in boats. Maybe it was better than being a dogsbody on a battle-wagon.

In 1940, my last year at school, I had joined a First Aid Unit. Later that year, at London's King's College, which had been unwisely evacuated to Bristol, we had fire-watched through the Bristol blitz, and my parents' house had been destroyed in the heavy raids on Plymouth in April, 1941. They had fortunately been safe in the Anderson shelter, and kind farmer friends had helped them salvage their furniture and found a cottage for them. I had hurried home from Bristol just in time to see a lorry coming up the hill as I approached our street, with my mother sitting beside the driver, holding the budgie in its cage. In the back, amidst the remains of the furniture, my father reclined in his favourite armchair. I leapt on board beside him and we joined a long trail of refugees, in lorries and carts and pushing barrows, which became denser as we reached the Torpoint ferry and crossed into Cornwall. The experience seemed quite unreal, just like the pictures we had seen of France the year before, which we had never expected to be repeated in our own home town.

My father, who had lost a brother at sea in the first war, on his twenty-first birthday in fact, must have watched with some anxiety when I left to join the Navy in January 1942. It was a sunny, spring-like day when I left the green slopes of the Tamar valley behind me and headed for *HMS Royal Arthur*, on the East coast at Skegness. On my arrival I was amazed and horrified. Butlin's former Holiday Camp at Skegness turned out to be in the grip of an arctic winter. Snow drifts covered the flimsy chalets, the swimming pools were frozen solid and the roads were inches thick in ice. I had never experienced anything like it before. Snow was rare in Devon and seldom lasted the day. On the first night, in pyjamas, under two blankets in the most exposed chalet nearest the sea, I shivered the hours away. It would be many months before I wore pyjamas or undressed completely again.

I had joined as a Writer but within a few days I had exchanged the Writer's 'fore and aft rig' for an Ordinary Seaman's 'square rig', having been advised that it would be to my advantage to become a 'CW candidate'. This meant doing a period of training and seatime as an Ordinary Seaman with the prospect of eventually qualifying as an officer. About thirty of us with the necessary educational qualifications were formed into a special class under the charge of kindly old Chief PO Shepherd – an apt name – who instructed us in Seamanship. There was also a likeable martinet of a Gunner's Mate, dapper and demanding, who set out to transform us into a squad of automatons on the parade ground.

It was a spartan existence, evidently designed to accustom us to the rigours of life on Arctic convoys. No scarves or gloves were allowed. We had to handle frozen rope ends and ice-cold rifles with bare hands as we learnt to tie knots, splice ropes or slope and present arms. And we learnt to keep our feet on the slippery roads whilst marching with the utmost precision. We spent our nights on fire-watch on the roofs of the dining halls, one of which was burnt out, although not by enemy action. Life was made enjoyable, however, by the cheerful company on trips into Skegness to visit the pier ballroom or the public baths. A hot bath became an indescribable luxury since the camp provided only wash basins with cold water in the freezing ablution blocks. These were, it's true, partially heated by coke braziers, the only source of warmth in the camp, permanently surrounded by crouching figures, huddled as close as they dared, smoking their home-made 'ticklers'.

These were cigarettes rolled from the duty-free tobacco, one of the Navy's most valued perks, which was supplied, at an absurdly low price, in sealed half-pound tins resembling the large tins of Navy jam from the Tickler's jam factory in Grimsby. At the first opportunity I obtained a tin of the pipe tobacco and hastened ashore to buy myself a pipe, determined to be a real sea-dog. I spent the evening in the Skegness Methodist Church canteen, puffing away beside a warm fire, until the potent fumes took their toll on my unaccustomed senses. I turned a luminous green and was so ill that I was never able to strike a nonchalant pose with a pipe again. Like everyone else in those unenlightened days I rolled my ticklers on a Rizla machine.

Another step on the path of experience was the ride back to camp on the late bus, when the air was filled with ditties in a language never heard during my sheltered upbringing. As the years passed, the war became a great linguistic leveller, accustoming the ear to habits of speech unknown before and long since cast off again. At the time, somehow, it relieved the tensions under which we lived.

The highlight of our training at Skeggie was a trip to Leicester, to provide a guard of honour at a ceremony to mark War Weapons Week. After spending a night in the stand at Leicester race-course, we were paraded in a suburban avenue. Standing smartly at attention in the front row, I was horrified to see two grinning faces only a few feet in front of me, which I recognised as belonging to two former schoolmates, still at University in the city. For the whole of the march through the town and throughout the ceremonial drill in the centre, I had the close, unsettling company of these two hilarious hangers-on. I shook them off when we were taken to a restaurant for a meal and my pal Basil Cudlippe-Green and I later found a night spot where naval uniform proved a rare and irresistible attraction. Basil was distinguished not only by his exotic name but also by his elegance and skill as a professional ice-skater. I encountered him again after the war, when he was a lead performer in the London Theatre.

After ten weeks or so of concentrated drill, I was given the awesome responsibility of taking a draft of seamen to *HMS Raleigh*, for further training. We managed to make it without mishap to Plymouth Naval Barracks, a familiar place to me, since I had been in and out of it in 1940, trying to teach spoken English to the French seamen who came over after the fall of France. I now found myself sleeping on the floor of the Gymnasium, the very place where I had helped my brother, then a PT Instructor, organise the Frenchmen's lessons. To add a second irony, we were transferred next day to Trevol, a holding depot on the Cornish side of the Tamar, where I slung my hammock on the rows of metal bars which I had helped my father devise in order to cram as many bodies into as small a space as possible in the cramped, decaying buildings.

Soon, however, we were installed at *Raleigh*. Obviously there was no limit to the perfection in arms drill which was required if a seaman was to be fit for duty on board ship. *Raleigh* was one huge parade ground on which we marched and counter-marched endlessly under the eagle eye of the redoubtable Chief PO Fenton. As we formed squad, left-inclined and right wheeled, we could see the endless line of exhausted, rifle-carrying figures struggling to run at the double round the perimeter, penalised for some minor infringement of the Chief's sadistic code of conduct. Even the cockroaches, which we saw coming out in thousands when on fire-watch in the kitchens, seemed to be marching in formation.

A group of us did, it's true, cross over to the Barracks occasionally for more technical tuition, principally in 'anchors and cables'. We gathered around a large, impressive model of a battleship's bow section, complete with the capstan and all the network of chains and shackles by which the anchors were made fast or lowered. We became expert in the complicated procedures by which we might one day be required to control the mooring of the *Rodney* or the *Nelson* – an awesome prospect!

I actually enjoyed the stay in my home port, being able to spend weekends in the country cottage where my parents had found temporary accommodation since the blitz. But soon I was ready to take my finely-honed skills to a sea-going vessel, and I received a draft-chit for Scapa Flow, where I was to join *HMS Echo*, a destroyer of the old E and F class, likely to be a little cramped for moving to the right in threes.

The war-time journeys from Plymouth to Scapa must remain vivid in the memory of many a serviceman. Long hours in crowded, not very clean, ill-sprung compartments, with that raw, unpleasant dryness in the throat caused by an atmosphere of mingled body odours, cigarette smoke and soot from the engine. Lengthy, unexplained stops. Fitful snatches of sleep, broken by an early morning turn-out for breakfast at some dark unidentified station. Then on again to Carlisle and a mass trek through the town for sausage and mash at the WVS canteen. Another night of crawling through the Highlands until a cold grey dawn lights the misty hills and it's everybody out again, to hump kit-bags and hammocks down into Thurso, for bacon and eggs courtesy of the Church of Scotland. Then on to the pitching boat for a first sight of the Old Man of Hoy and a queasiness in the stomach which seems to bode ill for the future, although it could perhaps be merely the effect of the journey.

On arrival at Lyness, the huge Scapa shore base, which provided all the necessities for the enormous fleet which filled the waters of the Flow, I was first sent to *HMS Tyne*, the depot ship, which put to sea for a few hours once a month to qualify its crew for duty-frees. Most of the destroyer flotillas were at sea, so I found myself transferred to the hulk of the old 'Iron Duke', beached near Lyness and used as temporary accommodation. The empty casements, where the subsidiary armament had been, were fitted with tables and benches and bars for hammocks, which gave raw recruits a chance to get used to shipboard existence without the added discomfort of a ship's motion. It was like a living museum of life in the old navy of my grandfather's day. To wash, you descended into the bowels of the ship, where you stepped through a door into a huge enclosed tank, awash with about three feet of hot water, steaming like a sauna. You could take a dip and dhobey (wash) your clothes at the same time. The 'heads' were literally in the ship's heads, or bows, as they were in past centuries. They were fitted into the outward curving flare of the bow in such a way that the seats were raised on a step up from the deck in a long row, so that the occupants sat like chickens on a roost. There were small partitions, but no doors, so that you looked along the row of bared thighs for a vacant throne to which you then ascended to join your shipmates. That provided yet another inhibition for a landlubber to overcome.

The *Echo* and her companions still remained at sea, so my next move was to a small transit camp in a couple of Nissen huts on the island of Flotta. This was a haven of rest run by an elderly Lieutenant with a very relaxed routine. By rights, of course, we should have been keeping ourselves up to the mark with morning divisions, drill and square-bashing, although the rough terrain would have caused a few problems. All we had to do was square up the hut each morning and prepare the meals. Then the day was free. Entertainment was provided by the Church of Scotland canteen and the large hall where the big ships' crews came ashore for ENSA concerts. On most days the canteen was frequented by local crofters, tall, lean men with long gaunt faces and black straggly hair, who hammered out Orkney reels all day on the battered piano. We did, however, enjoy an ENSA concert for the crew of the *King George the Fifth*. I chiefly remember the rousing reception given by the sex-starved matelots to an attractive young girl who sang 'Whispering Grass' with great effect. I think it was here, too, that I heard for the first time the one-legged baritone who seemed to haunt every ENSA concert I ever attended, and who always sang the same song: 'Water-boy-oy-oy, where are you hi-yi-ding'. I wished he could have found him and spared us further suffering!

At last the fleet came back. Rumour had it that there had been some kind of disaster in

Northern waters. We did not know then the full, sad story of Russian convoy PQ 17, unwisely ordered to scatter with the consequent loss of almost all its merchant vessels. I was ferried aboard *Echo* and stowed all my belongings in a locker on the crowded port mess-deck. Almost immediately we put to sea again, southward bound for the docks at Hull, where the ship was due to undergo a refit. By the time we got there, within a day or two of my joining, I had already lost my brand new oilskin coat, finding in its place an old buttonless wreck, held together with a piece of old rope. Then, when the port watch was given shore leave, I discovered that my cap had vanished, which meant that I was improperly dressed when I went to fall in for libertymen's inspection. I was in a catch 22 situation: I needed to go ashore to buy a cap, but I needed a cap to go ashore. It was a salutary introduction to the harsh reality of lower-deck existence amongst the hardened old salts with years of seatime behind them. A borrowed cap eventually solved the problem, but I was more wary from then onwards.

I was consoled by the thought that I would soon be sent home on leave for a week, perhaps two, since the *Echo* was to have a full refit. However, my hopes were quickly dashed. The *Tartar*, a Tribal class destroyer, was just completing her refit, so it was decided to transfer me to her without delay. I was joined by two other young hopefuls named Doug Galloway and Bill Park. Doug was a fair-haired, confident young lad from Blackpool, whilst Bill was a short, dark, very quiet Welshman. We soon became friends, finding it necessary to stick together in the face of the aggressive banter of the long-service 'skates' who formed the majority of our mess. We found that, quite naturally really, soft young rookies aiming for the quarter-deck were not regarded with much respect by hardened two- and three-badge ABs, who siezed the opportunity, while it was available, to get a little of their own back at the expense of the potential officer class. It was, on the whole, what might be called a profitable learning situation, which gave an insight into traditional attitudes and ways of thought and knocked a few soft edges off us. We learnt, as cook of the mess, to make 'clacker' (dough) and slap an awning on a pie, and rustle up a pot-mess (stew) or prepare a fanny (mess-kettle) of rich, thick 'kye', a kind of cocoa, made from condensed milk and naval issue slabs of hard, dark chocolate. As sick bay cleaner, I became familiar with the unpleasant diseases which could strike any seaman who failed to pay proper attention to hygiene, either ashore or afloat. We did also get some useful tips from the PO in charge of the tiller flat on splicing and painting techniques which served me well for long after the war.

Within days we were back at Scapa, going out with the Home Fleet on exercises to fit the flotilla for work as escort destroyers. The Tribals were comparatively modern, well-equipped vessels, which earned a high reputation during the course of the war at sea. They had two twin 4.7" gun turrets forward and a twin 4" high angle turret and twin 4.7" turret aft, as well as multiple pom-poms and torpedo tubes amidships. They had depth charges of course, and during the refit a number of 20mm Oerlikon cannon had been fitted, firing tracer, incendiary and armour-piercing shells. These machine-guns caused a great deal of speculation. What kind of job did they have in mind for us? Where were we going to be sent? What extra danger required these additional armaments?

For the time being we made the most of our opportunities for runs ashore. Scapa Flow at that time, with a host of battleships and cruisers, both British and American, was a bustling, crowded anchorage. Boats of all sizes criss-crossed the water, carrying ammunition, mail and stores, ferrying libertymen to and from the vast Lyness base, with its huge, crowded beer-halls, its canteens and cinema. The long jetty seemed to be always crowded with American seamen, with their white pork-pie hats, serge jackets and narrow, flared trousers, waiting for their big, grey cutters to take them back to their ships. There were oil-tankers, water-tankers and depot ships, and long lines of sleek destroyers, bright with camouflage paint. It was quite a thrill to sail past the towering bulk of the *Nelson*, the *Rodney*, the *KGV* or the *Duke of York*, familiar

HMS Tartar's rugby team, Scapa 1942. Henry Durell in white jersey. Author 3rd from right, back row.

from pre-war boating trips on the Hamoaze at Devonport. Now it seems strange to realise that the age of the battleship is dead and the empty Flow will never see such activity again.

I can still picture the scene as we accompanied the *Rodney* and *Nelson* out to sea on an exercise: their great grey silhouettes, with the long bows and massive gun turrets, standing out against the long low shore of the islands, the Old Man of Hoy behind them, lit briefly by sunshine as the fresh breeze swept patches of dark cloud across the sky, and the white spray glistening on the green waves between us. It was on days like this that I learnt to get my sealegs. I remember the first few times I had to struggle to lash up my hammock and stow it in the forepart of the mess-deck, fighting the effect of the nauseating rise and fall and sideways lurch of the deck beneath my feet. I can still recall going up to the galley to fetch a tray of baked tomatoes and staggering back with it, trying to concentrate on keeping it level, whilst my head reeled. I just managed to get it down the ladder and dump it on the table before rushing back up to the heads. No dinner for me that day! But thankfully I soon adjusted to the sharp motion of a destroyer in a choppy sea.

I found myself conscripted into the ship's rugby team for games against other members of the destroyer flotillas, alongside the awesome figures of the chaplain, the doctor and the First Lieutenant, who rejoiced in the impressive name of Henry Dumaresq-Durell. I, like most of the others, was a rather thin, brittle figure, but we had the advantage of possessing a group of five extremely brawny New Zealanders, who had all the skills and ferocity of the All Blacks. Whenever we got the ball all we had to do was to pass it to one of these and together they did the rest. I think we were undefeated in the few games we managed to play before duty called us elsewhere, and we found out exactly why we bristled with those Oerlikons.

CHAPTER 3

Malta Convoy

Towards the end of July, all hands were set to work, loading stores and ammunition for what was obviously going to be a long trip. On the 31st, we slipped from the buoy and found ourselves escorting the *Rodney* and *Nelson* westwards past the Old Man of Hoy, out into the Atlantic and around the Western Isles. We knew this certainly wasn't an exercise when we found ourselves joining up, two days later, with an impressive fleet which had sailed from the Clyde. A number of cruisers and destroyers were gathered protectively around fourteen large, fast merchantmen, the cream of the Merchant Navy, their light paintwork gleaming in the summer sunshine.

As we sped South together, through calm seas, with only the occasional report of a distant submarine or exercise manoeuvres to interrupt the relaxed routine, the war seemed very far away. I remember vividly the sense of luxury I felt as I spent my off-duty hours lying sunbathing on the fo'c'stle, sharing a tin of apples bought from the NAAFI. I would watch the flying fish leap from the sparkling sea or look admiringly at the smart, sleek lines of the ships of the convoy. But this was, in fact, 'Operation Pedestal', and our skipper, Captain St John Tyrwhitt, informed us over the loudspeaker system that our job was to fight these ships through to Malta, at that time desperate for aid and close to surrender. Little did we know how few of them were going to survive, but we knew now the reason for those guns!

Down in the mess-deck the old hands began to recall previous convoys which had fought their way through to Malta, and the casualties they had suffered. The atmosphere was sober, but still optimistic, and the games of 'uckers' (Ludo to most people) and 'Brag' became more intense and absorbing. I remember developing a sentimental streak, listening with greater interest to the songs which were continually played over the loudspeaker system:

'Yours, till the stars lose their glory,
Yours till the birds fail to sing'
or
'Never in a million years, will there be another you'.

I was writing at the time to my Bristol girlfriend, whose thick wool scarf – mostly knitted by her mother – had reached me in Scapa. But thoughts of the folks at home were strong, and I was regularly thrown into bouts of nostalgia by a frequently played baritone solo entitled: 'When the home bells ring again lad'. The threat of danger stirred very simple, basic emotions.

The day before the main force were due to pass through the Straits of Gibraltar, we sped on ahead to refuel under cover of darkness at the Rock. After the years of blackout it seemed strange to see fires blazing on the African coast and the brilliant lights of La Linea on the Spanish side of the bay. In the misty dawn of August 11th, we rejoined the convoy, now through the Straits, and were amazed to see how the fleet had grown. In addition to the battleships there were now four aircraft carriers, *Eagle*, *Furious*, *Victorious* and *Indomitable*, the latter not yet off the secret list, and the cruisers *Nigeria*, *Kenya*, *Manchester*, *Cairo* and *Charybdis*. The *Furious* was due to fly a number of Supermarine Spitfires off to Malta and then return, but the remainder kept due East at fifteen knots.

The calm water of the Mediterranean was like 'a witch's oils', full of reflected colours in the fierce blaze of the sun. Oblivious to the dangers ahead, we rigged up a hose on the after deck and cooled ourselves, dashing under the cascade of sea-water. But a rumour had gone round the ship that some lights we had seen in the early morning had belonged to some Spanish fishing vessels and that by now our presence would be known to the enemy. Indeed, all too soon we were made aware that our 'holiday' was over. I was in the mess-deck, having dinner before going on the afternoon watch, when one of our mess-mates came down the ladder and announced, almost casually, 'The *Eagle*'s gone.'

We hurried on deck, unable to believe his words. There, perhaps a mile off our port quarter, the big aircraft carrier lay heeling over at 45 degrees, the port side of her flight deck already under water. Whilst nearby destroyers went to rescue survivors, the main fleet did an emergency turn and sailed on. Within minutes she had disappeared.

At action stations I had the misfortune to be, together with Doug Galloway and another seaman, in the after shell-room, serving Y turret, the twin 4.7" guns on the quarter-deck. This was down in the bowels of the ship, below the ward-room. The narrow hatch, through which we three loaders squeezed to climb down into our steel prison, was screwed down above our heads, so that escape, if we were hit, was extremely improbable. We had to take the heavy shells from the racks and load them into a mechanical hoist which took them up to the guns. We could only deduce the course of the battle from the intensity of the gunfire, the demand for shells and the feel of the ship's manoeuvres, and our degree of apprehension fluctuated according to the intensity of the sound from guns and engines.

Our mate, Bill Park, had the job of taking the shells from the hoist as they reached the upper deck and passing them to the guns' crews. We had made him promise that if the ship got hit he would shout down the hoist to warn us and do his best to see we were freed from our prison in the shell-room.

'Oh yes,' he said, 'I won't let you down.'

When not at action stations, I was a bridge lookout, so that I had a brief view of approaching danger before the alarm bells sent us running to serve the guns. From our position on the starboard screen we had a magnificent view of the majestic array of big ships and one had to resist the temptation to stand and gaze at the huge pyrotechnic display as the guns opened up and the sky filled with exploding shells, through which the glowing tracers rose in curving lines, whilst the attacking aircraft came in low over the water. My memory of the next two days, as we ran the gauntlet of the Axis forces in the narrowing corridor past Cap Bon and into the straits of Pantellaria, is like a series of brief film clips of attacking aircraft interspersed with periods of tension down below in the shell-room and of comparative calm when night brought temporary relief, at least from air attack.

I have a vivid memory of the sky filling with the black shell-bursts of the massed guns of the fleet as a Blohm and Voss flying-boat, known from its shape as the 'flying shoe', came over on reconnaissance that first afternoon and then lingered menacingly on the far horizon. In the evening attack I remember a Savoia Machetti torpedo-bomber screaming overhead at mast height as I ran aft to the quarter deck. Another time I watched through my glasses a torpedo bomber speeding from outside the screen straight towards me, low over the water. As I shouted a warning to the gunner on the starboard bridge Oerlikon just below me, he directed a stream of cannon-shells straight into the nose of the plane and sent it crashing into the sea in a plume of spray. Then I rushed to my place in the shell-room, working frantically to keep the supply of shells rattling up the hoist while the guns barked above us in rapid bursts. I have a very clear picture of an attack on the afternoon of the 12th when, as I searched the sky over the fleet with my binoculars, a long line of tiny specks appeared flying in perfect order, high above the aircraft carriers. Suddenly the leader went into a steep dive, followed in turn by each speck in the line, straight down towards their target. As they straightened out and sped away, huge clouds of smoke billowed from the *Indomitable's* flight deck. Then, whilst everyone's attention was drawn to the Stuka dive-bombers, the torpedo bombers came in skimming the sea from each side, launching their torpedos into the heart of the convoy.

On the evening of the last day, as the big ships turned away to the North, leaving the rest of the convoy to face the difficult and dangerous task of negotiating the narrows, through to Malta, an even fiercer attack developed. All I saw of it was an enormous cloud of smoke and showers of sparks as the cargo of ammunition in an unfortunate merchantman exploded just ahead of us. Rushing down to the shell-room, we worked like demons, slamming the shells into the hoist whilst the deck above shook with the concussion of the guns. Then, suddenly, the rattle of the hoist stopped. There was silence above us. The churning screws below us began to race as the ship's speed increased and we clung to the racks as the *Tartar* heeled over to starboard in a steep turn. There came a sharp thump, as something seemed to hit the keel immediately beneath us and the deck heaved beneath our feet. Then the engine revs reduced, we regained an even keel and still the deck above was silent. Had the ship been hit, we wondered. Where was Bill? Had he forgotten his promise?

'Hello! Is there anyone up there?' we shouted up the tube of the hoist.

It seemed an age before Bill's voice at last called down to us.

'Are you all right down there?'

'Yes,' we shouted, 'what's been happening?'

'It was a torpedo,' came the reply.

'Where did it hit, are we sinking?' we asked anxiously.

'No, it missed,' he answered.

Bill explained afterwards that someone had spotted a torpedo track heading straight for the stern and they had all run forward, whilst the Captain had taken emergency avoiding action! It seemed as if the torpedo must have hit the keel with a glancing blow and failed to explode: if it had, we should mercifully have known little about it. But we didn't have much faith in Bill after that.

It was possible, on the other hand, that we had felt the shock of the explosion of a second torpedo, which had hit the destroyer ahead of us, *HMS Foresight*. It had blown off her stern, and she lay motionless a few cables away. We were called up to help with taking her in tow, while the tide of battle moved away to the Eastward. As we hauled away at the heavy manilla rope which had been made fast to the *Foresight's* bow, there came a loud 'whoosh' overhead and a column of water rose in the narrow space between the two ships. A stray Junkers 88 had swooped down on us whilst we were otherwise engaged. As we struggled to make the rope fast again, there came another aircraft alarm. This time, however, we recognised with relief the pointed wings of a Spitfire from Malta.

At last the tow was secured, but progress was virtually nil. As darkness fell, we were all summoned to heave at chains and ropes in an effort to fasten the ships together, side by side. We tended the straining lashings all night as *Tartar* struggled to make headway, but the first dim light of dawn showed that we were still close to the island off the African coast which had been visible on the previous evening. During the middle watch, the dim shape of another stricken ship had loomed up in the darkness and silently disappeared: perhaps the last sighting of the doomed cruiser *Manchester*, which was lost that night off Cape Bon.

We were still a sitting target for hostile aircraft, and we could do nothing now to aid the few remaining ships of the convoy which, with the badly damaged tanker *Ohio*, were straggling into Valetta harbour, so orders were sent to finish off the *Foresight* and return to Gibraltar. The remainder of her crew were taken aboard and we stood off and put a torpedo into her amidships. As she settled down and slipped below the surface, we headed West at full speed.

My next task was to go to help the doctor in the Sick Bay. The torpedo hit on the *Foresight* had killed the Commissioned Gunner and some of the after gun's crew and others on the quarter deck had been flung into the air and badly wounded. I had to help straighten the legs of one poor fellow and strap them into metal splints. The saddest sight was that of another who, blinded and battered, was thrashing about in agony and had to be tied into a bunk with bandages so that the Doctor could attend to him.

When everything possible had been done for the wounded, who lay on stretchers in the Wardroom flat, I found myself detailed to look after a German airman whom, at some time during the previous day, we had acquired in error, thinking he was a British pilot. With the help of a German dictionary, supplied by the Chaplain, I attempted to get as much information as possible from him, although I was hampered by the attentions of members of the crew, who proved remarkably charitable towards their nervous and bewildered enemy. I was obliged to keep at bay numbers of inquisitive shipmates who thrust cigarettes and chocolates on this new object of interest, as he sat with me in the corner of the Captain's pantry. It was interesting to watch his terror when the ship's guns opened up, presumably on a stray reconnaissance aircraft: he firmly believed in the power of his comrades to annihilate

Torpedo fired from Tartar to sink HMS Foresight – Operation Pedestal 1942

any British intruder into the Mediterranean. But he was more terrified still when we reached Gibraltar and his eyes were bandaged preparatory to his being taken ashore under guard. The sound of the escort's heavy tread and the clank of their rifles set him trembling with fear and he left like a man going to his execution! He must have been greatly relieved when he found how humane his captors really were.

During the next few days, as the battered ships of the fleet returned, Gibraltar was crowded with matelots working off the stresses of the previous week. As we were obliged to berth at the coal wharf, and we were compelled to wear our white Mediterranean uniforms, most of my shipmates presented a sorry sight after rolling back unsteadily to the ship from a run ashore. And as there was only a narrow plank between the ship and the quay, quite a few ended up taking an unexpected bath!

When the remains of the escort fleet had reassembled, and the damaged cruisers had been roughly patched up, a convoy was organised for the return to the UK. Although the cruisers *Nigeria* and *Kenya* had both been torpedoed in the bows, they were able to make quite a reasonable speed and to survive a full gale, which battered us as we went through the Bay of Biscay.

I remember a night watch spent as starboard bridge lookout, when we rolled so continually and so violently that for much of the time I was either standing on the side of the bridge, as if it was the deck, or clinging on to the rail to avoid sliding off to the port side of the bridge. When I went at last down to the mess-deck, there was water slopping from side to side as the ship rolled and no-one had been able to sling a hammock. We had to wedge ourselves as tightly as possible on the lockers between the mess table and the bulkhead and try to sleep, which, since we were so tired, was actually possible.

Being tossed about so unpleasantly made it difficult to prepare meals, and to find the appetite to eat them. This made it easier to put up with the problems caused by the breakdown of the refrigeration system, which meant we had no fresh meat or bread and had to manage with whatever the overburdened NAAFI could supply.

At last we arrived safely at the Clyde where, much to our surprise, every ship manned the side to cheer us as we passed on our way up the river. For a brief spell we felt like heroes. However, the Admiral's greeting, when we returned to Scapa, was very different: noting that we were still covered with Gibraltar coal dust, he sent one brief signal:

'A clean ship is a happy ship.'

So, instead of being covered in glory, it was hands turn to, on overalls and scrub ship! We were due for a boiler clean, which should have meant an opportunity for a day or two's shore leave. Even at Lyness, or preferably Kirkwall, that would have been welcome, but we spent the time chipping paint from the rusty parts of the deck and sides, so that we could earn the Admiral's approval.

When I did get an hour or two on shore, the thing which gave me the most pleasure, after a visit to the cinema and egg and chips in the canteen was, of all things, a visit to the barber's shop. The sensation of having one's hair cut and shampooed and feeling civilised again, after the weeks of blocked ablutions and infrequent changes of clothes was incredibly luxurious! For others, of course, the beer halls had an irresistible attraction after such a dodgy do and so much time at sea. The long jetty, where English and American matelots waited for their liberty boats, was the scene of frequent fights and headlong plunges into the chilly waters of the Flow. But after all the opportunity to relax and forget the war was all too short, as we were about to find.

CHAPTER 4

Slow Boat to Russia

We looked with surprise and apprehension at the clothing with which we were being issued. Here we were, just back from our heroic action in the warm Mediterranean; we had scrubbed and chipped and painted, to make the *Tartar* spanking smart again; we had toiled to reload with stores and ammunition; and we felt we deserved a decent spell ashore to taste to the full the fabulous delights of Scapa's Lyness recreation halls. But now they were dishing out fleece-lined waterproof coats, thick sea-boot stockings, mittens, balaclavas and jerseys, as if we were off again on some sort of polar expedition. Surely it couldn't be . . ?

It was. The announcement came as we put to sea again: another convoy for Russia! Everyone had heard tales of the ill-fated PQ 17, virtually annihilated after being ordered to scatter because the *Tirpitz* was thought to be at sea. Now the Tribals were off to defend PQ 18, bound for Archangel.

Soon we were fuelling in the picturesque and peaceful fiord of Akureyri, in the north of Iceland. We looked longingly across the calm, dark water at the pretty little town, with its gaily painted houses, in a variety of bright colours, lining the steep hillside. But we were not allowed ashore. Next day we were off again to join the convoy, which had come up from the Clyde and was now headed towards the dangerous waters around Bear Island.

There was some comfort to see, in the middle of the lines of ships, – some thirty all told – the AA cruiser *Scylla*, in which Admiral Burnett was flying his flag, and the ack-ack ship *Ulster Queen*, with the 'Woolworth' carrier, *Avenger*, to provide air cover and hunt for U-boats. There were extra Hawker Hurricanes specially fitted for catapulting into the air from one or two of the merchant ships as well. They were brave men who flew those planes, for they were almost invariably destined to ditch in icy seas. We heard, too, that strong units of the Home Fleet were not far away. But we were obliged to crawl along at the painfully slow speed of five knots. One old coal-burner, belching smoke from her tall stack, looked hardly capable of making even that speed. Although it was summer and the Arctic ice had retreated, enabling us to keep further to the North, we were still within range of the enemy air bases in Norway. The weather was fair, there was no darkness to hide us, and we were sitting targets for submarines.

On September 13th, only a day after joining the convoy, we had to watch helplessly as two large vessels were torpedoed and sunk. One of them, the American liberty ship, *Oliver Elmsworth*, lay only a few cables to port, and we could see the precious aircraft lining her upper deck, which now would never reach the Russian front. She slipped quietly into the calm, ice-green sea as the escorting destroyers sped around, searching for the intruder and dropping depth-charges in the hope of crippling him. Everything seemed calm and peaceful again an hour or two later, when suddenly the first air attack swept in. High level bombers came over first, trying to divert attention from the torpedo bombers, which skimmed the water, attacking from all sides and even hurtling down the lanes between the ships, causing their gunners to hit each other in the general confusion. Down below in the shell room, feeding the shells into the hoist, I saw little of the action, but Bill, my 'oppo' up above, told me of the agony of watching survivors from stricken ships drifting by, calling for help, whilst we, unable to stop, were forced to leave them to be picked up, if they were incredibly lucky, by the rescue ship astern. That first attack was disastrous: eight more merchant ships were lost. But, thanks to the *Avenger's* gallant squadron of fighters and the shooting from the AA ships and escorts, the enemy did not get off lightly either. Some were shot down and others damaged, with a long flight to face over an icy sea to a tiny wooden runway enclosed by mountains. A bomber ace, named Werner Baumbach, who led his squadron against PQ 18, wrote later, in *The Broken Swastika*, of the strain his pilots suffered under the unfavourable Arctic conditions, and the effect on their morale of finding the improvements which we had made in air cover, ack-ack defence and radar protection. They had thought that the break-up of PQ 17 had been due to the loss of nerve in the officers commanding the convoy, under the pressure of their air attacks. It was, of course, ordered by the Admiralty, where it was thought that the *Tirpitz* was at sea. They were surprised to find us daring to run the gauntlet again and even more surprised and disillusioned when they found the convoy was so well defended that many of their comrades failed to return.

This explains why, as time went by, our confidence gradually increased. Three further raids, at roughly hourly intervals, were driven off without loss, because they were not pressed home with the same determination, and we were able to slip away to Spitzbergen, going in line ahead up the fiord to where oilers were waiting to refuel the destroyer escorts. As we sailed up the narrow cleft between the barren cliffs, almost covered with snow and ice, the war seemed suddenly to have stopped. There was time to watch with interest the ice sheet cracking and breaking away from the edges of the glaciers, to fall into the fiord and

USS Oliver Elmsworth, first casualty of PQ 18, September, 1942

Tribal Class destroyers entering Spitzbergen, PQ 18, 1942

join the small icebergs drifting in the still waters. The men leaning over the guardrail of the oiler greeted us with a casual wave and I remember saying to myself, 'Morituri te saluamus'. It was a piece of schoolboy pretentiousness rather than a genuine awareness of the dangers they accepted so casually. However, we were to be given solid evidence of the particular risk they ran, through being so defenceless and so essential to the convoy that they were priority targets for submarines.

Next day, after we had rejoined the slow-moving convoy, there were four more air raids. But only one ship was hit, by a purely unlucky chance, because now the bombers were keeping high up in the cover of the clouds and dropping bombs at random. They tried these tactics again unsuccessfully the following day, by which time we were drawing out of range and also the weather had begun to close in, bringing freezing fog and flurries of snow. I now found myself 'promoted' to masthead lookout, since the danger now was from submarine attack. Every half-hour of the four hour watch, another seaman and I had to exchange duties: the relief had to climb the swaying wire ladder to the crow's nest, hanging out over the sea as the ship rolled heavily on her slow progress. He then had to climb up onto the protective cover above the crow's nest and wait while the man being relieved squirmed out, before squeezing back down into the lookout position. All this was far from easy as, to keep out the freezing cold, I had pulled seaboot stockings over my trousers, and put on two extra jerseys, my thick 'Bristol' scarf and the heavy fleece-lined coat, all of which did not allow much flexibility. Nor did the thick fleece-lined gloves allow a very firm grasp of the wire stays. Half an hour was quite long enough to stand, numb with cold, in the narrow platform, with snow blowing around your head, trying to pierce the mists ahead for the sight of a surfaced submarine. We made thick, hot kye, for each other in a big mess-kettle. How welcome it was at the end of each freezing half-hour!

I never did manage to spot a surfaced U-boat, suddenly revealed by a gap in the fog. One afternoon, however, when I was port bridge look-out, I thought for a few moments that I had earned fame and commendation. As I swept my binoculars over the pearly grey surface, I suddenly caught sight of a plume of water, running parallel to the ship's course, close off the port beam. A periscope! At last!

'Periscope bearing Red 90,' I cried excitedly.

There was immediate activity on the bridge as the First Lieutenant, Henry Dumaresq-Durell, called the Captain and sounded action stations.

Then, from all round the ship, the cry was repeated:

'Periscope to starboard!'

'Periscope astern!'

There were periscope plumes everywhere! We seemed to be in the middle of the Wolfpack!

Captain St John Tyrwhitt reached the bridge and took one look. Then he gave us a scornful glare and growled contemptuously, 'Whales!'

Furious at being disturbed by a crowd of idiots, he retired to his sea cabin below the bridge, whilst I tried to make myself indistinguishable from the signalling lantern on the port superstructure.

On the 17th the escort left PQ 18 to make its way into Archangel and transferred to a homeward bound convoy, QP 14. The German air force had had enough, but their subs took up the hunt. They chose as their main target the oilers on which we depended for fuel, and three were hit, in addition to the little sloop *Leda*. One, the *Grey Ranger*, with its tanks almost empty, refused to sink, so *Tartar* had to pump shells into her to finish her off. I can still picture her grey bow rising vertically above the flat grey sea's surface and then sliding slowly, gently out of sight. Ships so often seemed to accept their fate with such quiet dignity!

It was a dangerous time when a destroyer was manoeuvring slowly to pick up the hose from the tanker in order to fuel at sea. Once it had been hauled aboard and connected up, the two ships had to proceed together very slowly whilst the oil was pumped across, making them sitting targets for a submarine. On the 20th September, we had just finished fuelling from one of the tankers and pulled away to allow the *Somali* to take our place, when a sub, which had crept undetected into a firing position, released its torpedo. Unfortunately, it caught our sister ship amidships and put the engines out of action without, however, sinking her. She was taken in tow by a salvage tug and a valiant effort was made to get her to Iceland. Unfortunately, some days later a tremendous icelandic gale blew up. We and the convoy were by this time safely past Bear Island and heading towards home. The Somali, however, was still far from harbour and the force of the wind and sea was too much for her. She broke her back and sank, taking with her the members of her salvage crew. There was a grim silence on the mess-deck when the news came over the intercom and it made our own safe return to Scapa a sad, rather than a jubilant occasion.

A month or so later, in the security of the officers' training establishment at Hove, I learnt just how personal this tragedy had been. The charming nurse who was attending me at a blood donor session, learning that I had recently left the *Tartar*, proved anxious to learn more about the convoy. She revealed that the officer who had volunteered to go back to the *Somali* to try to keep her in tow had been her fiancé. I thought of what might have been the feelings at home if that torpedo had been fired just a few minutes before and had hit the *Tartar*.

CHAPTER 5

Coastal Forces

This was the experience of action to which the admiral had referred at my interview. Soon after the *Tartar* had returned to Scapa, we CW candidates, having completed the required period of sea time on the lower deck, were drafted back to barracks. Even though we had been based on Scapa for only five months, it was strange to see trees and women again. We seemed to have been in a quite different world.

Henry Durell, the First Lieutenant, must have left the *Tartar* not long afterwards, for he obtained a command of his own, the destroyer *Isis*. I was sad to discover, after the war, that he had gone down with his ship when she was bombed during the invasion period.

We soon realised we were back in the real world when we were sent to the training centre at *HMS King Alfred*, in Hove. It was drill and more drill, to bring out our powers of command and enable us to demonstrate our 'OLQ' (officer-like qualities). Our class was, however in the charge of Roger Hill, captain of the destroyer *HMS Ledbury*, which had earned fame during Operation Pedestal by bringing the damaged tanker *Ohio* into Malta harbour. He managed to keep a sense of proportion in our studies and there were intensive courses in signals, navigation and seamanship which gave us a good basis for our future careers.

A week or so after the admiral's vetting, on the 1st of January, I exchanged my bell bottoms for a Sub Lieutenant's uniform, purchased at their Lordships' expense from Austin Reed, and proceeded on a series of courses designed to fit me for the adventurous – and probably short – life of a First Lieutenant in Coastal Forces. We practised torpedo attacks at night at *HMS Vernon*, in Portsmouth, were terrorised by the ferocious but excessively respectful Gunner's Mates at the Whale Island gunnery school, and then studied more navigation at Greenwich Naval College. There we were reminded rather forcibly that there was still a war on, as we sat one morning listening sleepily to a navigation lecture, by a sudden roar, a shadow swiftly passing the window and a huge explosion which filled the room with dust and smoke. We piled out of the room and down the stairs in record time, only to find that our instructor, despite his age and corpulence, had beaten us all to it.

'Is everyone all right?' he enquired nervously, as he emerged out of the dust cloud at the foot of the stairs.

We had been the victims of one of the 'hit and run' raiders with which the Nazis were trying to keep London on the alert. The bomb had hit a section of our block, killing an elderly Captain who was ill in bed.

The following Sunday, we had just returned from an evening on the town when the sirens sounded – a fairly unusual occurrence by then. As I hurried, in my new No 1 suit, to my fire-watching post on the roof of the Wrens' block, the guns opened up and the old familiar uneven throb of enemy aircraft engines began to grow close. Reaching the parapet, I could see the searchlights and bursting ack-ack shells over the city. Then a loud swishing sound, remembered from the blitz years, heralded the fall of incendiaries, which showered over the College. These had explosive charges, for one crashed through the slates close to me and burst, sending flames shooting out of the roof. I picked up a sandbag, intending to pour sand on the fire, only to find that the rotten sacking fell apart, leaving its contents at my feet. There was nothing to do but turn and go down to the upper floor and join the fire-fighters directing hoses on the flames, whilst turning a blind eye, as far as possible, to the Wrens streaming past us in their night attire.

Next morning I went back to find my best cap, which had been blown off by the bomb. It was lying by the pile of sand at the edge of a large gap in the parapet, blown away by the explosion. In the darkness it had been invisible and I shuddered to think what my fate would have been if I had rushed forward with my sandbag. I decided it was much safer at sea.

After that, the course at the Coastal Forces training base at Fort William, in Scotland, was more like a holiday in a yachting marina. There were aircraft recognition sessions and ship-handling exercises on the loch by day and eightsome reels with the locals at night, while we speculated on what kind of appointment awaited us at the end. I was surprised and puzzled to receive instructions to proceed to Immingham, near Grimsby, to join some strange vessel known as an RML.

Early in May, after taking the opportunity to visit relations in Glasgow on my way, I found myself standing, with my kit-bag and cases, on the old iron bridge in Grimsby. This was the terminus of an interesting combination of tram and electric train, which passed through the town's streets before joining a railway line leading to Immingham Dock. We came to know it affectionately as 'the Clickety', from its peculiar rattle and bump. As it pulled up close to the dock, I was intrigued and a little apprehensive, wondering what the future held. I found a drab collection of huts, cranes and dock basins connected by cinder tracks and railway lines. A large lock allowed ships to enter and leave the river Humber at the varying states of the tide.

I was directed by the dock police to a basin where a number of rows of 'dolphins', or concrete pillars with mooring rings, ran out from the bank into the black, oily water. Connected to them were lines of floating catamarans, which provided a means of access to the vessels moored bows on to the dockside. In large figures on the bow of one of these craft I saw the magic number: 547.

A number of black, decaying Nissen huts stood on the waste land beside the basin. They held stores, ablutions of a rather primitive nature, a bare recreation hut and an administrative office. Much later, when I returned home on leave, I was surprised to discover that, by a strange coincidence, my grandfather had spent the 1914–18 war here. He had been an Armourer in Victoria's navy and had been recalled from retirement to service the guns of ships using the dock. Now I stood where he had stood, twenty-five years before.

I walked along the line of 'cats' and climbed the mediterranean ladder fastened to the side of 547. It was obvious that she was basically a standard 'B' type, Fairmile ML, such as had been used for training at Fort William, but there was a large box-like construction on the after deck. I made my way aft to the wardroom hatch and went down the companion. Two surprised faces looked up at me as I knocked at the open wardroom door.

'Sub Lieutenant Rowe reporting,' I said awkwardly.

'Oh yes,' replied a dark-haired Lieutenant, 'reporting for what?'

'I've been appointed here as First Lieutenant,' I replied.

The other officer, a sandy-haired, bearded Scot, whose name proved, predictably, to be Sandy, reacted with even greater astonishment than his skipper, who asked me to enter and explain this unexpected announcement. I, of course, knew no more than the brief statement of my appointment. However, I was offered accommodation and Mick Innes, my new CO, made enquiries at the naval base beside the dock, to discover exactly what the situation was. In the end, Sandy's new appointment came through and I found myself installed in his place as 547's Number One.

'Mick' proved to be a very efficient, helpful commanding officer. However, I had scarcely begun to learn from him the tricks of my new trade when he, too, was suddenly transferred to Combined Operations, the Navy's latest growth industry, in preparation for the various landings being planned in the Mediterranean and elsewhere. His replacement turned out to be Lieutenant Dick Olivier, none other than the brother of the famous Larry. He was a short, bearded, jaunty figure, extremely charming, with a liking for entertaining his friends with lengthy sessions of poker and scotch.

'Carry on, Number One,' was his favourite expression. Unfortunately, Number One had not had time to gain much experience, and not being able to get much sleep, since we lived, ate, drank and slept in the single wardroom and my bunk was occupied, until all hours, by his drinking partners, I was not too happy.

Neither of us knew much about the job we were supposed to be doing, carrying out Air-Sea Rescue operations in the North Sea. We knew nothing about the techniques of carrying out searches, or methods of contacting or working with aircraft. On the few occasions when we encountered an aircraft it appeared to be incapable of answering our signals, either by Aldis lamp or by wireless, and our few searches proved equally frustrating. Within a couple of weeks, Dick, who had come from the more adventurous and convivial life of the MTB flotillas, had decided that this boring and uncomfortable life was not for him. After a week of late night sessions he staggered up to the MO's surgery and arranged to be temporarily beached. I was to meet him again twelve months later, at Dartmouth, happily installed on the bridge of one of the powerful 'D' class MTBs, looking like one of the old Elizabethan seadogs.

So now 547 acquired another skipper, Lieutenant T.D. Andrews, better known to most of us as 'Andy'. We were destined to remain together until the end of the war, striking up a friendship which is still strong today, despite the tensions which could arise from time to time on a small vessel with cramped accommodation and few amenities. As Andy was senior in length of service as a Lieutenant to the other COs of the flotilla, he took over its command, so that we became the leading boat when at sea and responsible for the navigation and the organisation of searches. Andy had been a keen yachtsman before the war and had a natural feeling for the sea, as well as an ebullient personality which quickly established amicable relations with colleagues.

Andy was keen, too, to overcome the difficulties we had been experiencing in collaborating with the RAF and to establish an efficient rescue service. Thanks to his efforts we quite soon began to obtain results, as the stories of our rescues show.

CHAPTER 6

The Skipper's Story

by Andy Andrews

For me, it started in 1940, when, at home with my wife and small son at Wanstead, Essex, we heard the sound of German guns firing at Dover.

We realised that the war was getting too close and that my job as Clerk of Number Two Magistrates' Court at Stratford, London, could turn into running the court under the Nazis. I decided that I would rather do some more active war service, although I was in a reserved occupation.

By the strangest coincidence, that very week-end the radio announced that yachtsmen were wanted immediately for the Royal Naval Air-Sea Rescue Service. The immediate rank of Petty Officer was offered for experienced yachtsmen and, since as a youth at Southend-on-Sea I had had a small half-decked sailing boat called *The Auk*, which I had sailed in and around that area, I considered I knew how to sail. With a mile of mud-flats at Southend-on-Sea at low tide, one had to be able to cope with the elements to get back to one's mooring! I had certainly learned how to cope with the tide and to respect the sea and the weather.

I volunteered and, within a few days, was told to report to the Royal Naval Reserve base at Lowestoft.

That was the week-end that London was very heavily bombed and the Thames seemed to be on fire. Not only were bombs coming down, but flak, and also bombers that had been hit by flak.

I was certainly relieved to be leaving for Lowestoft but, on arriving there, I was put before what seemed to be an Admiral, judging by his gold braid, who wanted details of my yachting experience, yachting employment or Yachtmaster's Certificate.

My meagre experience did not impress him, but I managed to answer one or two testing points and, when he realised that I had made up my mind, he slid me through. What he was really looking for was experienced yacht masters to take command of beautiful yachts which the Navy had taken over. This was also the base where experienced Merchant Navy personnel were taken into the Royal Navy. I was neither, trying to be both!

That day I was signed on as an Ordinary Seaman and the next day I was promoted to Petty Officer and drew a Petty Officer's uniform. Thus I never had a seaman's uniform as, until then, I had been wearing my civilian clothes.

The third day I had to parade in my Petty Officer's uniform and was promptly put in charge of a bunch of seamen for the parade. All I could do was watch the group in front and give orders to do the same, but about three quarters of a second late! Off we marched to class, and I was sitting there quite interested while a Chief Petty Officer was showing us how to strip a Lewis machine gun.

He had cleverly removed the butt by pressing something into it, when the door opened and a voice called:

'Petty Officer Andrews.'

It didn't ring a bell with me, of course. A second call and everyone turned to look at me in my uniform, and I woke up to the fact that it was me. I was told to report to the Drafting Master-at-Arms, where I found a queue at a ticket window. When my turn came I was told:

'You are appointed to the command of *Lady Pam*. You will join her at Fleetwood. Your seaman will join you at the station and your engineer will follow tomorrow. Here are your papers.'

I turned away in a daze, when another Petty Officer ushered me into a corner with about twenty others who were likewise dazed. He held up a board with the insignia of rank of all the officers of the Army, Navy and Air Force and ran through these with short explanations, showing us how to salute in the RN fashion and advising us on some of the foreign services, who wore lots of braid but were not commissioned officers. Then we were sent to pack our gear and meet at the station.

I was in the Navy now!

At the station I noticed a huge crowd of seamen approaching in a tight bunch. Someone reported that it was my seaman and then I could see that they were in a literally tight bunch, because they were propping him up. Then they poured him into the carriage.

Apparently he was a genuine sailor, a broad Scot, who wore medals from the First World War and had been recalled. His papers had been 'mislaid' at the base, and he had been there for several weeks, so that, when it came to a send-off, all his friends had certainly sent him off!

The journey from Lowestoft to Fleetwood is an easy cross-country run, but that was not the way the railways ran. They ran North and South, so it meant 'North a bit' and change, then 'South a bit' and change, and so on. My problem at the first change was that I had my kit-bag and suitcase and my seaman had his kit-bag and suitcase, but he was absolutely out! Fortunately I found a porter with a trolley and said,

'Please transfer this lot on the trolley to the next train.'

This accomplished, I could sit down and begin to think. What do I do in this situation? What is the drill? Have I any powers of punishment? This chap has served through World War One, so he will know everything, so I must get off on the right foot.

Then I suppose that my experience in the Magistrates' Court came to my aid. In the morning he had recovered, after being sick a couple of times out of the window, and he apologised and said it would not happen again, but it had been the set of circumstances when he had left. Anyway, I talked to him like a Dutch uncle, although he was over twice my age, and then said that the incident was best completely forgotten. I am sure he wouldn't mind me repeating it now as, after that, he really was a marvellous sailor and would quietly and unobtrusively suggest a better way or say something in Naval terms, so that I wouldn't make a bloomer as a Petty Officer, due to my lack of training.

Reporting at the Naval Base at Fleetwood, I was told that the *Lady Pam* was afloat in the dock, and that I was to get her out and on to a railway wagon and trans-ship her to Swansea, South Wales. Quite simple, really, if you've done anything like that before! So, once again, into the breach dear friend, and I ordered a twenty-ton crane, spreaders to prevent the wires cutting the hull in half, and a flat-bed railway wagon, and in no time we were in a train headed South and passing *Lady Pam* following in a goods train.

My engineer had by now joined and he was also a Petty Officer and came from Scotland. Thus, with a Scottish engineer, a Scottish seaman and myself, half Scottish, we were ready to take them all on.

At Swansea, having reversed the process and put the *Lady Pam* back in the water, we started our Air-Sea Rescue service. *Lady Pam* was a high speed, hard chine speedboat, with a seat for the driver and another six-foot long fore and aft seat, on which a casualty could be placed. This was all in a small wheelhouse, open to the rear. Amidships was quite a large, powerful engine, under cover, and aft of that was a small cockpit for three passengers. Its job before the war had been to take passengers for a ride round the pier for a shilling.

Our equipment for Air-Sea Rescue was minimal. We had no radio. We had a signalling torch, but I had not yet learnt Morse. We had a compass, so that if we did go out one way, at least we could come back on the reciprocal. Eventually we got a local chart. We had a few runs out along the coast towards Mumbles, to try the engine and the boat. We did carry one rifle, but the problem with that was that the wheelhouse was not tall enough to shoulder arms, and I felt it would not look right standing up to shoulder arms in the cockpit!

The problem about Air-Sea Rescue was that all the action was taking place at the Dover end of the Channel, and nobody had told the pilots that we were at Swansea, just dying for them to fall into the water.

Eventually we were transferred to Barry Island, South Wales, where we lay at the outer jetty of the harbour, ready for immediate Air-Sea Rescue action. We had to man a telephone there and await a phone call. Then we were to dash out into the night. We begged that telephone to ring. We would repeatedly check to see if it was working. No joy!

We were joined by a Royal Air Force Rescue Launch, which shared our watches, and which allowed us to go ashore in turn for a few hot dinners, and some nights to sleep. Life on board was very frugal and chilly, but we were ready to do our Air-Sea Rescue if only it would happen! We were even afraid that when the RAF took over we would miss our chance. Still the war did not come to us.

Eventually I was invited to take the Admiral's wife out for a run when I was doing an engine check, so that revived our spirits a bit. I didn't know, of course, whether to take her hand to help her aboard or salute.

After a few weeks I was told to report to the docks to unload into the harbour an American tunny fishing cruiser, which had come across the Atlantic as deck cargo and been sold to the Navy for one dollar. This was to prevent it being a gift and infringing America's neutrality.

It was over 70 feet long, a huge high-speed motor launch, with an enormous engine, saloons, an upper bridge, then a monkey bridge on top of that for observation, and then a look-out above that, and it seemed to tower into the sky. My job was to make a detailed schedule of alterations that would have to be made to make her into a sea-going ASR launch. With the vast experience of Air-Sea Rescue which by now I should have had, this should have been no problem but, once again, I could only start at the beginning. So I started my paper-work by naming her *Questor*.

My report duly went in, but I never saw her in action because, before her refit could be completed to turn her into a real ASR launch, and to be my pride and joy as I had designed her, the Commander called me to the Base and said that I was being sent for a commission.

So far I had learnt 'Port' and 'Starboard', 'Fore and Aft', doing 'Colours' at sunset and a little Morse code in case an aeroplane tried to contact us after we had left the telephone. Thus the greenest Petty Officer ever to arrive at Lancing College began his Officer Training.

Lancing College, in West Sussex, close to the coast between Brighton and Worthing, was a wonderful old public school which had been taken over by the Royal Navy for turning out RNVR officers. It was set in its own grounds and had an atmosphere of learning and tradition which immediately had its effect on those who arrived there.

The rule in the Navy was that you had to serve three months at sea before you could be sent for a commission. This normally meant service in a destroyer, battleship, or similar real Naval ship, with officers, Chief Petty Officers and so on. That way, at least, you could learn about Naval routine and Divisions and rum.

One consolation for me was that as 'Officers in Training' we wore a white band round our caps, and whether we were Petty Officers or seamen did not matter. All we had to do was learn the whole Naval system of navigation, gunnery, torpedoes, submarine warfare, aircraft recognition, anti-aircraft combat, parade control, drilling, uniforms to wear in different situations and so on and so on. A thousand years of tradition crammed into three hectic months. We even had to do night sentry duties to guard the school against possible enemy attacks or just 'exercise attacks'. Never a dull moment.

Most of my private catching up had to be done sitting in the privacy of the smallest room!

I found that trying to catch up on 'square bashing' from a Training Manual did not seem to fit my brain. 'From the halt to the halt on the right form squad', which is where you shuffle round from a standing start to a new position round the corner where you stop, never seemed to get to me. However, all the time we were told that they were looking for 'OLQs' – officer-like qualities – but we were never told what they were, so we could not relax for a moment.

On one parade, where we were being marked for our command of a squad being drilled, I had stood rigidly at attention as each of the squad in turn went out in front to demonstrate a certain movement and then give the command. Finally my turn came and I was told to demonstrate and give the order for 'Ground arms'. This entailed taking the rifle up in one hand and doing a full knees bend, back straight, rifle ready to lay on the ground, but I was so stiff that I slowly fell backwards on to my behind while the rest of the squad fell about laughing!

'Here's a fine how-d'you-do,' I thought. So I picked myself, and my rifle, up and in my strongest voice said,

'Attention! Stop all that laughing. That is not the way to do it. If you have stood rigidly under orders for too long, that is bound to happen.'

By now, I had eased my muscles, so that I was then able to give the proper demonstration and recover my composure. I can still feel that awful moment.

After Lancing College we transferred to HMS King Alfred, which was the swimming baths complex on the front at Hove, for more technical training, and finally came the day of the passing-out parade when we got either our stripe or a railway ticket. I was very satisfied to come 11th out of a group of 72, having regard to all the ground I had to catch up.

At the time of my passing-out, there was a call for volunteers for the SOE. Fortunately I did not know what it meant, so I mentioned to my interviewing officer that I had joined as a volunteer for Air-Sea Rescue and had had command of a launch. He told me that now I was an officer I would have to obtain a watch-keeping certificate before I could get another command.

I was duly sent to Plymouth as a Sub Lieutenant and Number One of HM Motor Launch No. 1035, under a Canadian skipper, Lieutenant Baldwin. This meant that I was the first officer after the captain, but the trouble was that there were no other officers – no Number Two.

Our job was to patrol beyond Plymouth harbour, listening with Asdic for enemy submarines trying to penetrate the harbour where the big ships lay. Already tiny one-man and two-man submarines had penetrated our harbours in the Mediterranean and had done a lot of damage.

The Atlantic to the West of Plymouth was also being patrolled by huge Sunderland flying-boats, which took off and landed inside the Sound, and we had the additional duty, when they were taking off or landing, of standing by for Air-Sea Rescue should one of these giants crash on landing or take-off. Thus I was a part of another form of Air-Sea Rescue service of the Royal Navy. Fortunately there were few incidents, although, when they were taking off fully laden, and had only a very short run to clear the Breakwater and its fort, we always used to wait anxiously for the bang, because they were so close. I certainly admired the reliability of the work of their engineers and their pilots. On one occasion a Sunderland was forced to land outside the breakwater and was proudly towed in by the boat from our flotilla which was on ASR standby.

In the meantime I had been working for my watchkeeping certificate although I was, of course, already keeping watch on the bridge, turn-about with my skipper, and in due course I was the proud owner of a Watchkeeping Certificate for Harbour Defence MLs.

Also, by now I was promoted to Lieutenant RNVR and soon took over command of HDML 1035 when Lieut. Baldwin was transferred to fresh pastures. Thus I was now back to where I had been as a Petty Officer, except that I had a really fine boat under my command. These MLs were 72 feet long, with a well-shaped round hull, with a very good diesel engine, and packed with armament and depth-charges. In addition they carried an underwater Asdic dome and all the Asdic equipment in the wheelhouse for seeking and attacking submarines. I had had a course up in Scotland to train me in the use of this equipment and we also carried a trained operator.

The equipment was so good that we could detect a shoal of fish and thus we were able to augment our rations with a good catch of fish when it was convenient. So far as Air-Sea Rescue was concerned, we had plenty of stand-by but very little action.

My next appointment was to the Royal Naval base St Christopher, to commission ML 563, but very soon afterwards I was appointed to *HMS Beaver II*, which was the HQ of C-in-C Humber at Immingham, near Grimsby. I arrived there, as an 'additional officer waiting for an appointment', in May 1943. Within a few days I received orders to take command of RML 547 which was in the 69th Flotilla, consisting of four boats, RMLs 547, 553, 550 and 520.

RML 547 was under the command of Lieut. Dick Olivier, brother of the well-known Laurence, later Lord Olivier. Dick was somewhat unwell, but we had to spend the best part of a day going through and checking all the stores and equipment. Then there was a party, and he was gone.

That night I discovered that we were due to sail on Air-Sea Rescue patrol in the North Sea and also that, by virtue of my seniority as a Lieutenant, I was Senior Officer of the flotilla and we would be lead boat. I could see now why they had me standing by as 'additional officer'. No time was to be lost!

There was I in a strange boat, 110 feet long, with a strange crew and a strange river, at night, with virtually no navigation leading lights, amongst the wrecks of bombed ships, 'sailing down the river'. Fortunately my new Number One, Sub Lieut. Alan Rowe, had been down the river before and he was an extremely careful and accurate navigator, so we managed to reach the sea without mishap, despite my nervousness at every shadow along fifteen miles down the river. Thus I had now entered the real Royal Naval Air-Sea Rescue Service. These launches were specifically designed for Air-Sea Rescue, unlike the boats I had served on before, and my purpose in joining the Royal Navy would now be fulfilled.

The Naval ASR service had developed from private boats and yachts, which had been acquired and which were used with very little modification for Air-Sea Rescue, through to Naval Motor Launches performing other duties, with ASR as a sideline, to Rescue Motor Launches specially designed with a sick-bay for rescued airmen, with a Sick Berth Attendant and with Direction Finding equipment for homing in on aircraft or on portable transmitters in dinghies. In the next three years we were to play our part as the service developed still further in its organisation and efficiency.

CHAPTER 7

A Friendly Foe

Being off duty, on the day following our first rescue, did not mean we could take things easy. There was plenty to do cleaning ship and carrying out all the usual maintenance. There were the guns and ammunition to clean and check, charts to bring up to date, water and stores to replenish and engines to be serviced. Surprisingly, however, we were not called on in the next few duty days to put to sea on patrol.

At the weekend, our gunner, Harry Boswell, asked for leave to go to his home in Hull to sort out a domestic upset and, as the weather seemed unsuitable for air operations and on the Monday we were supposed to be on stand-down again, he was allowed a twenty-four hour leave. Harry, a former Hull trawlerman, used to 'swing the lamp' rather frequently, reminding us that he had taken part in the St Nazaire raid on the same ML as Able Seaman Savage, who had won a posthumous VC for standing by his gun under heavy fire from the shore batteries. However, this experience had made him proud of his guns, which he serviced with loving care. His post at action stations was the powered turret on the fo'c'sle, containing twin .5 machine guns. He was also responsible for maintaining the twin Lewis guns on each side of the bridge and the Oerlikon aft.

When Monday came, totally unaware of the destruction that had already been carried out and was still planned away to the east, I decided to take the opportunity to visit the bonded store to obtain our month's ration of duty-free tobacco and chocolate and order our wardroom spirits ration. Whisky, if I remember correctly, was six shillings (30p!) a bottle and gin four shillings and sixpence (22p!). We were obliged to entertain so many 'friends' that we drank little of it ourselves. So I set out early, catching the electric train into Grimsby. I spent the morning at the warehouse beside the docks and then, having a considerable load to carry, decided not to linger in the town, but to return to the ship.

It was fortunate that I did, for I was amazed to see, as I came through the dock gates, that two RMLs were waiting in the lock for the water to rise so that they could enter the river and put to sea. What was more surprising was the fact that the nearer one was 547, with Andy on the bridge and 520's number one, Dermot Barton, on the fo'c'sle, doing my job of supervising the handling of the mooring ropes! Just in time, as the lock gates were opening, I leapt aboard, whilst Dermot jumped back on to the dockside. Immediately, the ropes and fenders were hauled in and we made for the river in the company of RML 553. What had happened was that our two other boats had managed to develop engine trouble, leaving us to take over their duties, so no-one was in a very cheery mood as we left the shelter of the boom and cleared Spurn Point, meeting head-on the full force of the wind and the rising sea. We would have felt differently if we had known what the bomber crews had had to face, sent out that weekend in thunderstorms and severe icing conditions, to suffer unnecessary casualties in raiding a city already in ruins. It was for them a tragic finale to a week of slaughter and destruction.

However, knowing nothing of this, we forged our way through the mounting waves out to our waiting position by the Outer Dowsing shoal, and from midnight onwards spent an uncomfortable time, running up and down at slow speed, first into the wind and waves, then running before them, so as to keep more or less in the same place, holding on grimly to anything solid at the turns, as the boat rolled on to her beam-ends before coming round to a safer pitching motion. It was quite impossible to stop engines and heave to, as we would have rolled so heavily and been driven well away from our patrol position.

'Harry Boswell must be laughing his head off,' said Gower, the Coxswain, wrestling with the wheel as the bow dipped into a wave and a cascade of water drenched our little group on the bridge, forcing its way through the chinks in our oilskins and adding its quota to the chilly dampness which was seeping over our bodies.

'At three in the morning?' said Jock Wilson, a matter-of-fact young Scotsman, 'He'll be crashing his swede, like all those other lucky sods on shore.' (Crashing your swede was Navy speak for going to sleep.)

The middle watch was going all too slowly and uncomfortably. It came as a relief to hear Jim Cannon's call through the voice-pipe and to crawl down into the wheel-house to read the signal which he passed up through the hatch. He, poor lad, was forced to sit cramped in a tiny cupboard, with a bucket beside him in this weather, flung to and fro, straining to concentrate on the stream of morse which flowed continuously through his earphones. But he had managed to pick out our call-sign and to get down the details of the signal: 'Powered dinghies dropped in position 54.55N, 04.00E, proceed at once.'

With Andy taking over on the bridge, I had an equally uncomfortable time, jolted about in the wheelhouse, plotting a course which, allowing for wind and tide and the effect of weather on engine speed, would get us back north-eastwards to the same area in which we had been searching previously. Then this had to be passed to Roy Marshall, my opposite number on 553, by the night lantern, before we could set out, with them following our shaded stern light. Fortunately the weather gradually began to ease, enabling us eventually to make our normal fifteen knots, which meant it would take eleven hours altogether to reach the position we had been given. This was when we envied the fast boats, the MTBs and MGBs and the RAF HSLs, with their forty knots of speed, although it had to be admitted that none of them could have coped with the weather conditions we had come through. As the morning wore on, we thought of the men out there, buffeted by last night's storm, fighting to keep alive, desperately hoping that their dinghy, a minute speck in a vast expanse of sea, would be seen in time.

It was just after noon when Harry Ainsworth called from the crow's nest that a dark object was floating not far ahead. Putting on our few knots of extra speed, we raced towards it, only to find that it was part of the undercarriage of an aircraft, kept afloat by a large wheel. The weed growing on the metal spar showed that it was obviously not the victim of a recent ditching, so we had to leave it and press on, wondering to what unknown tragedy it bore silent witness. Could it have been associated with a previous search in which we had been involved? So often there were reports of dinghies at various positions, and searches were made only to be called off by the shore authorities with no further information as to whether survivors had been found or whether the report had been inaccurate. It was most depressing to be recalled to base with the question still in our minds whether there might still be men waiting in the depths of the sea, hoping in vain for rescue. As we were to find, through later experience, a dinghy could be seen by an aircraft and then lost again in darkness or bad weather, and it might take days and a lucky chance to find it again. At that time it seemed to occur to no one in authority that shared information and experience, and bringing everyone together to discuss their problems, would improve immeasurably the morale and efficiency of the service.

However, the prospects of success in this case seemed to be improving when we were

'Make and mend' – crew on fo'c'stle of 547. Left to right: Manks, Mason, Gower

given a change of position for our quarry. Although we had to go further to the North-East, it could only mean that daylight had brought a fresh sighting by search aircraft.

'Keep a good look-out,' said Andy, 'there must be a plane circling the dinghy. I hope 553's wireless operator is doing his stuff.'

Our own radio was tuned in to receive messages from headquarters, whilst 553 was keeping watch on the 500kc international distress wavelength on which search aircraft were supposed to communicate. If the search aircraft was carrying out the correct procedure, it would contact 553 when it received our call-sign, and start sending out a homing signal. RMLs carried a RAF direction finding aerial, which was housed in a cigar-shaped cover on the wheelhouse roof. If 553's telegraphist picked up the aircraft's signal, he would be able to take a bearing which would lead us to the dinghy. An hour went by with no result. Then 553's signal lamp commenced to blink.

'Hudson reports circling dinghy sixteen miles ahead,' I read, 'D/F bearing 025 degrees,' and I hastily calculated the new course, as we turned to starboard, with 553 following suit, at maximum revs, each eager to make the pick-up first.

Suddenly, as we drew nearer, not one aircraft but a whole swarm appeared, circling low over the water around us at all points of the compass. Some came swooping over our masthead, circled and then flew off in so many directions that we became quite confused as to which way we should be heading. We noted with surprise that there were Spitfires, Beaufighters and the new twin-engined B-25 Mitchell bombers. At last, we spotted a smoke-float, which seemed to be the marker for a dinghy, and 553, being the nearer, headed towards it. But just then a Mitchell came towards us and, for the first time, carried out something like the official procedure for guiding us to a dinghy. It swooped over our masthead, circled, and flew away eastwards in a straight line, rocking its wings as it did so. Andy promptly ordered a turn to starboard, following it at maximum speed. All eyes were now on the sea ahead, which fortunately was smooth and bright.

Clem Woodhead in the crow's nest was first to spot the tiny dark object. 'Dinghy bearing green one-o,' he shouted down to the bridge. Already our port boom had been hauled out at right-angles to the ship's side, and the scrambling nets attached to it were lowered. Ainsworth and Manks were standing by with heaving lines, whilst Tom Goodwin and Jock Wilson, in lifebelts, were preparing to climb down and help lift the airmen up on to our deck. We came gently alongside what we found was not a dinghy but an airborne lifeboat. This was a boat, about twenty feet long, recently designed to be carried flush with the underside of a Lockheed Hudson and dropped on parachutes. A specially equipped squadron of these aircraft had recently been formed to carry out Air-Sea Rescue duties, so that improvements in the organisation were, indeed, under way.

The three survivors were gently lifted up, via the rope netting, and carried the few yards to the sick bay aft of the engine room. They were exhausted from four days of rough weather, and suffering from cuts and bruises, so they were rapidly cleaned up and bandaged by Bowler, our Sick Berth Attendant. Then they were taken below and tucked up warmly in our wardroom bunks to rest and recover, whilst the boat was secured astern, to be towed back for re-use. We were to find out later that, although a few drops had already been made, we were the first to bring one of these lifeboats back after it had been dropped in a rescue at sea.

A rapid examination showed that the lifeboat was quite an ingenious invention. It had a slim, low hull and inflated yellow panels at bow and stern to give it buoyancy and provide shelter underneath which a man could lie. Beneath the thwarts were a series of lockers containing tins of food, water, cigarettes and petrol, down-filled one-piece suits, fishing lines, a radio transmitter and sails. There was a drop-keel for stability, a mast and oars and a small petrol engine. Everything necessary seemed to have been provided, although not everything always worked perfectly. The petrol cans had to be re-labelled 'Gas', after an American crew had been unable to work out what was meant by 'petrol'! The drop did not always work perfectly, as two large parachutes had to be blown open, one at each end, to bring the boat down on an even keel, and then released by a special mechanism, whilst at the same time rockets were supposed to fire life-lines out in different directions for the occupants of the dinghy to grasp and haul themselves to the boat. There can be little doubt, however, that the successful drop in this case saved the lives of the three survivors, even though they had some problems, as the account of their experiences in their squadron records reveals. It is worth quoting this in detail to show just what men had to endure to escape the dangers of ditching in the bleak North Sea.

226 Squadron, Aug. 5th 1943

If only this was a newspaper! This could make a centre page feature article. Banner headline, too!

Today there arrived at Swanton Morley three bruised and bearded men, recently landed at Grimsby off the naval launch which picked them up. They were F/O A.P. Eyton Jones, F/SGT D.W. Bishop, and SGT J.F. Lecomber. All had supper in the Officers' Mess, followed by much chinwagging.

The story they told me was this. On July 30th, their aircraft had been circling a dinghy at various heights, transmitting at intervals, when it was intercepted by 8 German aircraft, mainly Me. 210's. The pilot immediately headed for home as fast as possible, but the fighters caught up easily. The first attack was thwarted by turning into the attack, causing the enemy aircraft to overshoot. At this point Sgt E.R. Norburn, the top gunner, got in a good burst, registering strikes. The other enemy aircraft followed up, however, and pressed home the attack, mainly from dead astern. Both engines were hit and caught fire, and the fuselage, from the bulkhead back, was also alight. The bulkhead stopped a great amount of the enemy fire, but Sgt Norburn was killed by bullets in the chest. After the engines caught fire there was no alternative but to ditch. A really good ditching was not possible, because of the lack of height, and the aircraft hit the water at between 200 and 220 m.p.h. There were several bounces and then the aircraft must have broken up, because it filled and sank immediately. The pilot, F/O R.M. Christie, was either killed or knocked unconscious immediately on impact, as he made no attempt to get out, neither could he be got out. F/O Eyton-Jones (observer) has no idea how he left the aircraft – for what seemed like a full minute he was submerged, and then, suddenly, he felt himself leaving the aircraft. Judging from his multi cuts and bruises he must have burst through the astro dome. When he eventually broke surface he had been rising for some time, so the aircraft must have sunk considerably. The first thing he saw was his hat, which he still has – a salt-stained, shrunken relic.

Meanwhile F/Sgt Bishop and Sgt Lecomber had released the dinghy and, although they were initially trapped in the aircraft by radio equipment which had fallen on their feet, they succeeded in getting clear. (Through a hole which had not been there a few seconds before.) The dinghy was boarded and the crew rowed around among the wreckage, scavenging. They picked up a first aid outfit and three (single-seat) K type dinghies. They opened these last in order to be more conspicuous to searching aircraft. Then wet, bruised, cut and shaken, they waited, not particularly cheered up by the knowledge that they had only a few energy tablets and no water. Two Hudsons were seen by the crew when they first got into the dinghy, but the Hudsons were somewhat preoccupied as they were being chased by the German fighters. It transpired that they had seen the Mitchell ditch, however, and they subsequently reported its position.

After about three hours, more aircraft appeared, and during daylight hours from then on there were aircraft circling practically all of the time. One of these aircraft, the next afternoon, dropped an airborne lifeboat about a hundred yards away from the crew, and they were able to row towards it and climb aboard. They changed into dry clothing (which did not remain dry for long) and also found that they had more comprehensive rations. The engines were started, but both petered out after about three hours – this was due to the engine casing having sprung a leak when the boat was dropped. After the failure of the engines, sail was used and following winds and following seas were of great advantage in steering the course which had been flashed by Aldis lamp from the Hudson. The chief exercise consisted in trying to swing the engines back into life. In fact, both engines were stripped right down and reassembled, but with no success. A system of watches was devised, and this enabled anyone 'off duty' during the day to lie in the sun and dry his clothing. Unfortunately the weather was deteriorating, culminating in a storm which threatened to tear the sail to shreds and which snapped the rudder. F/O Eyton-Jones then decided to chop the mast down and tow it in the water as a form of stabiliser, but this was not particularly successful. Although there were some 'shaky do's', the boat did remain right way up. Rations during the period aboard the lifeboat consisted of nine Horlicks tablets, one tin of condensed milk and one tin of water per man per day. Each day aircraft appeared and circled and then disappeared. F/O Eyton-Jones once said "Just think – they will be home for tea" (and at the mention of tea morale dropped a bit). No. actually morale in the crew was very high, although some of the cuts sustained by the crew had turned septic and were very painful. (The first aid kit which had been picked up was ruined and useless.)

So things went on until, on Tuesday, 3rd August, some Beaufighters appeared, obviously guiding something towards the dinghy. The hopeful watchers waited and the hopeful waiters watched, and eventually they saw a mast appear over the horizon – before long two R.N. rescue launches had arrived on the scene, one of which picked them up. On board, the rescued men were given dry clothes and a cup of hot, sweet tea, the best they had ever tasted. Soon they were asleep.

The plain, matter-of-fact way in which these men's ordeal is described is typical of the stoical wartime attitude to danger. There is no mention of the effort which Eyton-Jones had to make to fight his way up towards the faint glimmer of light at the sea's surface. He told Andy how he had struggled to hold his breath until, unable to hold on any longer, his mouth opened uncontrollably in a huge gasp, which he believed would drown him. To his surprise, he found himself gulping in fresh air, as his head, just at that moment, broke surface. The storm, too, which we had found uncomfortable enough, had almost overwhelmed them. With the rudder smashed, they had been forced beam-on to the waves, which swept over them, filling the boat with water as it wallowed in the troughs. The drogue which they made from the mast and sail was carried away and it was not until they made another from their down-filled suits that they had some means of keeping head-on to the seas. For two days of storms they were forced to bale continuously to keep afloat, only sustained by their will to live and the knowledge that their colleagues were watching over them, as they saw the Mitchells come and go.

I calculated that our position was now 55.08N and 04.17E, well out into the widest part of the North Sea and nearer to the enemy coast than our own, which meant that we had to keep radio silence. Relying on the aircraft to report the rescue, we set course to the South-west, with the lifeboat in tow, which reduced our speed somewhat. Immediately the sky, which minutes before had been buzzing with aircraft, became completely empty, and we were left to plod home over a lonely, though tranquil sea. It had become a pleasant summer afternoon and we were feeling quite satisfied with ourselves and the way in which the rescue procedures had, up to a point, worked, although it was difficult to understand why it had taken so long to decide to send us to sea, when the men had already been drifting for three days and they had been circling another dinghy before being shot down.

'Those enemy aircraft could still be about,' said Andy, 'and all that fighter cover is well on the way back home. We'll keep everyone on deck on full all-round watch.'

For an hour or so we carried on, searching with our binoculars the distant horizon and the clear, empty sky. Then suddenly Ainsworth, the port lookout, reported aircraft approaching from the South. Small as they were, it took only a glance to recognise them as hostile. Low over the water, speeding towards us, were the sinister, bulbous-nosed silhouettes of two Junkers 88s, accompanying a large, ungainly seaplane, possibly a Heinkel 59, by the look of its large floats.

'Action Stations!' called Andy, as he pressed the alarm bell. Keeping his eyes on the approaching planes, he bent to the voice pipe. 'Cannon, make an enemy report to base: "Three enemy aircraft approaching". Number one, pass him our position. Manks, Evans, cast off the tow quickly and then man your guns.'

As they hurried aft, and the crew stood by our guns, I rapidly checked our position from the chart on the wheelhouse table and Cannon completed his signal. Then I noted our change of course as we swung to face the enemy bows on so as to make a smaller target and bring our .5 machine guns in the for'ard turret to bear. Immediately the awful realisation hit me that Boswell, our experienced gunner, was a hundred miles or more away, absent for the first time at the moment he was most needed!

Fortunately, without waiting to be ordered, Tom Goodwin, who had acquired a knowledge of the working of the powered machine gun turret, had leapt in and trained it on the approaching enemy. Jock Wilson had strapped himself into the Oerlikon aft, with Evans as his loader, and Manks and Woodhead had clipped magazines on to the twin Lewis guns on each side of the bridge and swung them outwards on their mountings. Meanwhile Doug Tratner, on 553, which had been astern of us, brought his boat well out on our port side, to present a wider target and provide combined fire-power. Where were all those fighters, we wondered, which had been zooming all round us such a short time ago. Just a couple of Beaufighters were all that we needed.

Our yellow decks singled us out as rescue craft, and our orders were to fire only if we were fired on first, as there was supposed to be an international understanding that rescue ships and aircraft should be immune from attack. However, our Mitchell crew had been shot down whilst on ASR duties, and we had no evidence of the Germans being prepared to observe this arrangement, so we expected the worst.

'Keep steady! Hold your fire,' called Andy, 'Don't open up till they do.'

The three planes loomed larger, streaking over the water towards us, whilst we watched, tense and anxious, guns cocked and fingers on the triggers, waiting to see the spurts of flame from the enemy which would be the signal to open fire.

As they came within range, the floatplane, covered by one of the Junkers, swung out to give us a wide berth to starboard, whilst the other Junkers came straight through the gap between our boats at little more than masthead height. He was so close that we could see into the perspex nose of the aircraft, where the pilot sat grinning down at us. With a friendly wave of his hand, he went past us and on and away, disappearing rapidly northwards with his two companions.

With an immense sense of relief, we picked up our tow again and resumed our course for home, thinking with amazement that there must have been very few who, like us, had come face to face with the enemy and exchanged a friendly wave and nothing more. Obviously, they were on a rescue mission too, and they were prepared to stick to the rules of the game.

The whereabouts of the dinghy which the Mitchell had been circling were still a mystery, so it was no surprise to receive orders to search around a new position further East, where a Halifax had reported sighting a dinghy. On arriving there, we proceeded to carry out a box search, from six in the evening until midnight. Frequently more aircraft were sighted, apparently also searching for the dinghy, but none came anywhere near us. The surface of the sea remained empty and no call came through on the rescue frequency as we went patiently round and round, covering an ever wider area of sea. At length, with darkness making any further search impossible, the recall signal came, ordering us to bring our survivors back to Grimsby, and so, with a certain degree of reluctance, we headed homewards once more.

Dawn on the 4th of August brought another alarm, as we spotted another Ju 88, which sent us to action stations again. This time, perhaps, we looked too dangerous for a single plane so far from land, for the aircraft circled us at a respectful distance and flew off again. It was late in the evening when we at last entered the lock gates at Immingham, and we were surprised to find a large gathering of officers and Wrens from the base standing on the dockside, anxious to ensure that we had returned without damage or casualties. Most of our servicing of depth charges, guns and other equipment was done by a very attractive group of Wren technicians, to one of whom Doug Tratner was already engaged. Others of us had become quite attached to some of them, too, and so, when the news of our enemy report got round, followed by a long silence before our ETA (estimated time of arrival) came through, there were a number of anxious hearts eager for news of our safe return.

'You never knew how much you'd be missed, did you sir?' said Flash, grinning as his eyes moved from one of the worried faces back to mine. From then on we certainly enjoyed much more respect and attention from our friends on shore!

But, although we had enjoyed a certain amount of success, we were still dissatisfied with the inadequacy of the Air-Sea Rescue system. RML 553 had been given the call-signs of a number of co-operating aircraft, but only one had made contact, leading us fortunately to the lifeboat. But there were obviously other dinghies in the area, which might have been found if the other search aircraft had known we were there and how to contact us. The Mitchell crew told us that they had no instructions to use the 500kcs frequency and they did not know how to liaise with surface vessels to home them on to a dinghy. An efficient organisation, ensuring on-the-spot communication between our boats and the RAF search aircraft, could have produced the rescue of the original dinghy on the previous Friday and avoided the suffering undergone by the Mitchell crew. We had to assume that either the men in the first dinghy had been lost in the week-end storms or they had been picked up by the German rescue service, perhaps even by the seaplane we had encountered.

Now, long afterwards, we know much more about what was happening during that hectic week called the Battle of Hamburg and in the month which followed. The Germans were obviously incensed by the amount of destruction and the tens of thousands of deaths which the fire-storm had caused. It was important, too, to capture American airmen in order to assess the tactics and capabilities of the forces being employed in the new daylight offensive. It must have seemed to them that they were in danger of losing control of their half of the North Sea. On July 30th, for example, a total of 111 allied aircraft were used for searches alone in German waters, and, in addition to the shooting down of the Mitchell, enemy fighters prevented an attempt to drop an airborne lifeboat to two American dinghies nearer the Danish coast. On the Saturday and Sunday, two more lifeboats were dropped in the area, by Hudsons with Beaufighter escorts. One of these was able to make good progress westwards and its three survivors were picked up by launches from Yarmouth, but the other vanished. Maybe this was the one we had been sent to search for after we had picked up the Mitchell crew.

This wasn't all, however. On August 24th, a battle developed between two American Fortresses and two Ju 88s, after a German message had been intercepted, indicating that a seaplane was about to pick up the occupants of an airborne lifeboat in a position 54.04N and 05.05E. The Fortresses shot down one Ju 88 and left the rescue plane burning on the surface of the water; they were then forced to leave because fuel was running low, after circling the boat for two hours. The Germans were thought to have moved in after this to rescue the survivors from all three planes.

Next day, in retaliation, two Hudsons were set upon by nine or ten Messerschmitt 110s after they had seen five men climb from a dinghy into a lifeboat which they had dropped. One of the Hudsons was shot down and the lifeboat was raked with machine-gun fire. A Stirling was also reported missing from ASR duties. When, however, three Hudsons, with an escort of eight P-51 Mustangs were sent to the area, only Danish fishing vessels could be seen.

So the repercussions of the battle of Hamburg carried on over the sea for some time, and shattered the fragile understanding which had existed between rescuers on both sides. We had been very lucky to have encountered an enemy who was prepared to observe the rules of war, because we had offered him first strike at a very vulnerable target. One burst of fire would have shattered our unprotected bridge and wheelhouse. A nervous finger on the trigger in either of our boats could have unleashed an attack such as was made later on HSL 2551, which suffered heavy casualties in trying to rescue an American bomber crew.

It seems all the more tragic to think that the smiling enemy, with whom we had shared a moment of mutual understanding, might together with his companions have been the victim of those American Fortresses, shown no mercy himself on his mission of rescue. Was that seaplane the same one as we had seen? What the Americans saw was an enemy aircraft asking to be shot at. They did not stop to consider that its crew were engaged on an errand of mercy, perhaps saving the lives of allied airmen. We, on the other hand, had seen our apparent enemy face to face and recognised in him a fellow human being. Personally, I have always been glad that for a good part of the war I had the privilege of saving life rather than taking it.

As we had a sandwich and a cup of cocoa before we turned into our bunks that night, Andy and I talked over the events of the past few days, reflecting on the efficiency of the rescue services and the partial, though welcome, improvement in communications.

'I was glad to see you turn up in time,' Andy said. 'I didn't feel at all easy about having Dermot as my navigator.'

CHAPTER 8

The Unsinkable Lanc

'Hell's bells! What do they think they're playing at?' yelled Jock's horrified voice out of the darkness, as the increasing drone of returning bombers was suddenly punctuated by the scream of bombs and the thunderous crash of explosions coming closer and closer, until they seemed to be all round us.

Lying, like sitting ducks, at our patrol position, wondering at the sound of aircraft so early in the morning, we were shaken rigid, as the saying was, to find a full-scale raid taking place all over our patch of sea, instead of being delivered where it ought to have been in the centre of Berlin. Crouching behind what little shelter the bridge provided, we waited in terror for the din to cease echoing over the sea. There was nothing we could do but sit it out and hope it would soon be over.

'I always thought the Brylcreem boys were pretty clueless at navigation, but not that clueless!' said Mac an hour later, when the hail of bombs had ended at last and we and 550 had come alongside each other to check we were both unscathed. Fortunately we were small targets and the bombing had been spread over a wide area, whilst the sea had, of course, reduced the impact of the bombs, but the mass of propaganda leaflets we saw floating all around us when daylight dawned showed how close we had come to a watery grave. We fished out a few to find that they were headed 'Luftpost' (Airmail!) warning the Germans of the fate which awaited them if they continued the war. Why on earth hadn't they been posted on the right target?

The only reason had to be that the raid had been aborted for some reason and the bombers had jettisoned their loads, as regulations required, at least eighty miles from the English coast, supposedly well away from friendly shipping, but regardless of the fact that this was just where we were expected to hang about! We did on other occasions hear bangs and see flashes on the horizon, which could have been the odd aircraft jettisoning its bombs, or more probably lightning, but this was a real thousand bomber blitz.

What was happening, in the latter part of 1943, was a determined effort by Bomber Harris to win the war on his own. After Hamburg, it was to be Berlin which got the treatment. The Americans, after their brave but costly daylight offensive, begun with the July raids, had been forced to reconsider their tactics. The success of the German fighter defences against, for example, the heroic attack on the Schweinfurt ball-bearing works on October 17th, showed that formation flying and the gun-power of the Fortresses were not as effective a defence as they had hoped. Harris, therefore, was going to maintain the attack single-handed, using every available aircraft, including training squadrons, to make mass night bombing raids into the very heart of the Reich, as often as the weather conditions allowed.

No-one told us, of course. We just sat out there as usual, in the middle of the sea, waiting and wondering. The heavy pasting we received that night, however, did give us some idea of what the enemy, particularly in Berlin, was having to endure, even though we were spared the thunder of the ack-ack batteries and the terror of the fire-storm, whilst the blast of the bombs and the sound of the explosions had been muffled by the sea.

The opening round of what was to become 'the Battle of Berlin' had started with two attacks at the end of August. These were followed by another on the night of September 3/4th, when the Germans used a new form of fighter direction to counteract the use of 'window', the aluminium foil strips which had given our planes such effective protection when first used over Hamburg. Using a continuous running commentary on the shape of the raid, the enemy were able to bring in their night-fighters to hammer the bombers on their homeward flight.

One of the dark shapes which flew ahead of us into the night on that September evening, as we steered our familiar course towards the East, was Lancaster C Charlie, of 106 Squadron, based at Syneston, Notts, and piloted by Squadron-Leader Howroyd. The outward trip was fairly uneventful and they had no problem in dropping their bombs on the target at 2339 hours from 20,000 feet. But the crew's relief, as they turned for home, was short-lived. Almost immediately they felt the aircraft shudder as cannon-shells and machine-gun bullets ripped unexpectedly into its fuselage. The rear gunner, Sgt Mackenzie, was hit in the first burst of fire and the bomb-aimer, Pilot-Officer Saxby, crawled from the nose of the plane to collapse, badly wounded, at the feet of the flight engineer. From his mid-upper turret, Sgt Kelly spotted their surprise attacker, a Me 110, dead astern and only 150 yards away. Opening fire, he called at the same time for the captain to corkscrew to port, so S/L Howroyd threw the Lanc. into an extended barrel corkscrew, rolling over first to port and then flinging the plane into a climb to starboard and over to port again. The manoeuvre took a full five minutes but, twist and turn as he might, the British pilot could not shake off the enemy fighter. With the rear turret out of action, there was no defence against an attack from below and astern, and this was evidently an experienced opponent. Four times he came in and scored hits in the port wing and centre fuselage. One cannon-shell hit the sight-bracket of Sgt Kelly's gun, sending pieces of metal flying into his mid-upper turret and wounding him in the right eye, but this did not stop him from returning the fire as the opportunity arose.

'How can we get this Jerry off our tail?' muttered Howroyd.

'Next time he comes in skipper, dive,' called Kelly through the intercom. Then, a few moments later: 'Dive now!'

As Howroyd threw the plane into a sudden dive, the surprised enemy, coming up from the rear, was slow to react and overshot the Lanc., presenting its underside at close range to the determined gunner, who poured his fire into the attacker. With grim satisfaction he saw the bullets smash into the Messerschmitt's engine and nose, sending it into a steep dive to starboard. From the side window, the wireless operator watched it continue its dive, with smoke pouring from both engines and fuselage.

In spite of the damage she had suffered, the Lancaster still responded to the controls, enabling Howroyd to keep weaving and corkscrewing as he headed for a gap in the searchlights until, at last, they were clear of the danger zone over the city and could resume level flight. To the crew's immense relief, the engines continued to run smoothly and the petrol tanks appeared to be undamaged, so they set course for home, doing what they could for their two wounded comrades. P/O Saxby, the bomb-aimer, had, however, been so badly wounded that he died soon afterwards.

As they neared the enemy coast, the pilot and engineer realised that the damage was worse than they had thought. Their petrol supply was decreasing rapidly and the tanks must have been hit, so that the chances were they would have to ditch before they could reach England. As S/L Howroyd nursed the aircraft homewards over the sea, the wireless-operator put out a mayday call, gave their position, and clamped the transmitter key down so that the shore stations could obtain a fix on their final transmission. The rest of the crew meanwhile made their preparations for the ditching and for getting the dinghy away. Finally, still some 200 miles from their base, the fuel tanks ran dry, the engines spluttered and failed, and the pilot brought the Lanc. gliding down to a perfect landing on a relatively calm sea.

Although the damaged nose broke open, the aircraft came gently to rest on an even keel on the surface of the water and, helped by the buoyancy of the empty petrol tanks, remained securely afloat. The dinghy inflated itself without any difficulty, and the five relatively uninjured crew members laid their badly wounded rear gunner into it, before climbing in themselves to await the result of their distress call.

They were fortunate in having been able to carry out the ditching drill with no problems from a crash landing or a rough sea; and their position was pretty accurately known on shore. All too frequently heavy damage and bad weather caused problems with the navigation and the ditching, so that the condition of the dinghy might be poor and its position very uncertain. Often, even if a good mayday position had been sent out, the aircraft might have travelled on quite a distance before it finally hit the water, causing obvious problems to the searchers. Surface vessels on their own had a very limited visibility range, so that an inaccuracy of even a few miles could make all the difference between rescue and failure.

In this case, Hudson ASR aircraft from Bircham Newton, in Norfolk, were sent out at first light and had no difficulty in spotting the Lanc. as it floated conspicuously near to the dinghy on a calm blue sea. An airborne lifeboat was sent floating down from one of the aircraft, on its large parachutes, and settled on an even keel close to the dinghy. The release mechanisms all operated correctly: the parachutes disconnected themselves, the rockets fired, and one of the lines which were shot out fell close enough for the airmen to pick it up and haul themselves to the lifeboat. Soon they were able to lie in comparative comfort on a solid deck, warm and dry in the down-filled suits and well supplied with cigarettes, chocolate and the other comforts which they found in the lockers. Meanwhile, one of the Hudsons circled continuously above them, sending out a homing signal on the distress frequency.

It was not long before Nore Command Headquarters called us on our waiting position giving us the position and the call sign of the aircraft. Immediately we were on our way, with 550 listening out for the Hudson's transmissions whilst we remained in contact with base for any further information. It was 1220 before we were close enough to pick up the aircraft's signals and steer towards it using our direction-finding dome. There were still another three hours to go before we would reach the lifeboat, and by three o'clock the plane had to return to base because fuel was running low, but two other members of the squadron took over and spotted us as we approached. One remained over the lifeboat, whilst the other came low towards us, circled and headed back towards the lifeboat, rocking its wings as a sign that we should follow.

'That's odd,' said Andy, as our objective came into view, 'there seem to be two lifeboats.' There were, indeed, two dark objects faintly visible on the horizon. 'Steer for the one dead ahead, Coxswain. 550 can take the one to starboard. Full speed ahead both.'

Bowling along at all our eighteen knots of maximum speed, with boarding nets and helpers at the ready, we soon came near enough to see what was lying ahead of us.

'It's not a dinghy, it's a Lancaster!' exclaimed Clem Woodhead, in amazement.

The Lanc. was still afloat, with both wings spread over the surface of the sea, and we had been sold a dummy. While Sheppard and MacLaren, on 550, closed the lifeboat and triumphantly hauled the survivors aboard, we went closer to the plane and lowered one of our Carley floats, which the coxswain and Tom Goodwin paddled across to the fuselage. Being low in the water, the float gave easier access than our sailing dinghy, and allowed them to look inside and check the plane thoroughly. On their return, they reported that the plane was empty. The body of the bomb-aimer must have been lost when the nose broke open on hitting the water.

On 550 the five survivors were soon made comfortable. Unfortunately the badly wounded rear gunner, Sgt MacKenzie, had died during the morning. It always gave one a sad, disheartening feeling, to see, laid silent and lonely on the after deck, the canvas-wrapped body of a man who only the evening before had laughed and joked with the lucky ones now safe and heading for home.

'Well, we can't carry the Lanc. back with us,' said Andy. 'It's a pity, but we'll have to sink it so that no one else spots it and starts another pointless search. You can have some target practice, Boswell.'

Getting into the for'ard turret, our gunner put burst after burst from the twin .5s into the tough body of the plane, but it appeared to have absolutely no effect. We brought the Oerlikon on the after deck to bear, but again the cannon shells did not do enough damage to make it break up. With no petrol in the tanks, it could neither burn nor sink.

'Stand clear for depth charge attack,' signalled Sheppard, before moving in to drop one of his depth charges, set to shallow depth, over the stern, as close to the plane as possible. A fountain of water obscured it for a moment, but then subsided to reveal it again, still obstinately refusing to go under. We tried more gunfire, still with no result.

'Well, we've got to get these chaps back to base,' said Andy at last. 'It can't remain afloat much longer. We'll take the lifeboat in tow and let 550 go on ahead with the survivors.'

After seeing the lifeboat secured by two ropes to our stern bollards, I gave Andy the course for home and left him to take the first turn on the bridge, whilst I enjoyed some supper and a doze in my wardroom bunk. I could feel the motion of the boat begin to increase as the weather, which had been so kind before, began quite rapidly to deteriorate. By nightfall a north-easterly gale was whipping up the waves, which came crashing against our starboard quarter, lifting the stern and making the ship corkscrew down into the troughs. Consequently, the lifeboat was flung towards the boat's stern at one moment and jerked back at the next, putting an uneven strain on the tow ropes. When I went back up to the bridge to relieve Andy, towards midnight, I found that they had almost lost it when one of the ropes snapped, making it yaw even more wildly from side to side. The coxswain and two of the crew had managed to haul it into the lee side of the ship and fasten another rope, despite the lurching of the boat and the rapid rise and fall of the waves.

Wedged into the starboard corner of the bridge, braced against the support of the signal lockers, I could see the white spray, which outlined the wave-crests against the pitch-black sky, rising high above our starboard quarter, it seemed almost to mast height, as Tom Goodwin wrestled with the wheel to keep the ship on a steady course. Down aft, drenched in spray, Fred Manks was struggling to follow the movements of the lifeboat and to make sure that the tow was holding. Inevitably, it was not long before we heard him shout that a rope had parted and, before I and Harry Ainsworth could reach him, that the other, chafed and strained by tugging against the bollard and the ship's counter, had given way too.

Two ropes' ends were now trailing and twisting from the stern of the boat, and threatening to be swept underneath and around the propellers by the surge of the waves, so the first priority seemed to be to avoid endangering the ship.

'Quick!' I shouted, 'haul in the ropes'.

Manks and Ainsworth speedily hauled them inboard, but the lifeboat had disappeared by now into the swirling black waters.

I sent Manks to inform Andy, who was quickly on deck beside me, not very pleased to find that his prize had vanished.

The floating Lancaster

Hudson aircraft dropping the airborne lifeboat

Airmen in the lifeboat, with the dinghy

Lifeboat alongside RML 550

'We'll turn about and search for it,' he said. 'Hard a-starboard, Goodwin. Ainsworth, man the searchlight.'

We carried a small searchlight on the side of the bridge, which was now directed at the oncoming waves, lighting up the curtains of flying spray rather than the murky sea. For what seemed like hours we pitched and rolled in the greatest discomfort, crawling to and fro in a fruitless search for the little boat. In the wheelhouse, striving to keep a plot of our movements on the chart, I was flung from side to side, together with my compasses and parallel rule, finding it virtually impossible to make a mark of any kind on the bucking chart table. It was a situation in which the harmony of our relations was decidedly strained. However, we received a signal at last from base, recalling us to harbour. To my great relief we abandoned our fruitless search, reaching harbour later that morning. Meanwhile, of course, the survivors had been landed and taken to hospital.

There could be little doubt that the lifeboat had been swamped and sunk eventually, and that the Lancaster too had been broken up by a storm of such fury. Neither was ever heard of again. But the aircraft must have come close to setting a record for endurance, after at least fifteen and possibly twenty-four hours afloat. This compares well with RAF records on the durability of the Halifax on which a study was once made. In eight ditchings the average time the aircraft remained afloat was 7 hours 32 mins, and the longest time was a remarkable 33 hours. Our C for Charlie might have beaten that if the weather had held, in spite of the pounding we gave it! It seems a pity that its broken frame has to lie out there now, deep beneath the waves, where the oil platforms stand and the tankers pass unheeding!

We received a letter of thanks from the Commanding Officer of 106 Squadron and we ourselves were pretty pleased to have at last participated in a really well co-ordinated operation which showed that ASR was being taken seriously, with improved equipment and procedures. Memoirs published since the war have shown that up till then stand-by Halifax crews from operational bomber squadrons had been used for ASR searches. They had had no proper briefing on communication with rescue launches, on radio frequencies to be used or on the procedures to be followed when launches were sighted.

Not before time, the top brass began to realise the importance to morale of persuading aircrews to pay attention to dinghy maintenance and ditching drill, because there really was a good chance of survival if they were forced to ditch on the way back to England. Andy had put in a number of comments and suggestions, in his reports on our operations, aiming at improving the rescue service, and consequently we were both invited down to the Nore Command Headquarters, near London, where we were able to see how the huge plot was operated which controlled all the operations on the East coast. We had a long discussion with the controller of the smaller plot which showed air operations and the disposition of ASR patrols. For the first time we were able to discuss each other's problems and help each other to understand and overcome our difficulties.

On our way back from London, we visited the base at Bircham Newton, in Norfolk, from which the newly formed Hudson ASR squadron operated which had performed so well in our recent rescues. They took us up on a practice flight, aimed at spotting a dinghy floating somewhere in the Wash. Whilst Andy sat up beside the pilot, I had the dubious privilege of standing with my head in the astro dome, holding on desperately to the airframe as we dived and banked and the horizon swam and swayed crazily above my head. To our surprise and dismay, our parachutes had been flung casually into the rear of the fuselage, but wearing one would have made no difference to our safety at the height at which we switchbacked over the sea. Of course, there was absolutely no reason to suspect that the aerobatics were put on especially for our benefit, or was there? But it convinced me of my wisdom in choosing the Navy, where you at least had a solid deck beneath your feet.

Later on, we visited a Lancaster base near Lincoln, where we were taken up on a navigational exercise over the greater part of central England, getting a useful idea of how it felt to fly in a Lanc. It seemed to have the slow, steady solidity of a London bus, and it was difficult to imagine it being flung around the sky in a violent corkscrew. We, in turn, gave hospitality to RAF crews, helping them to appreciate the efforts being made to ensure their safety and the value of effective dinghy drill.

Among our visitors were the survivors from our recent rescue. They were about to go back on ops, facing again the strain of flying into the increasingly efficient German air defences. I could sense the nervous tension which had been created by their recent experiences and the effort they were having to make to summon up the courage to continue their tour. We gave them a noisy lunch-time party in our wardroom, with plenty of duty-free scotch and gin, and wished them luck as their transport drove off from the dockside, back to duty.

I often wondered whether they survived their tour, as they so deserved to do after what they had been through. But it has taken almost fifty years to discover the sequel, thanks to the Bomber Command Association's research into the records of bomber losses. The crew must have been reformed, with replacements for the two men who were lost, for the records show that on the 8/9th October, only a month after the rescue, and perhaps just a few days after they had left us, Sqn Ldr Howroyd, Plt Off T.H. Davies (newly-commissioned), Sgt D.S.K. Chappell, Sgt A. Williams, Plt Off L.D. Cromb, F Sgt R.G. Kelly and Flg Off A.J. Horobin were shot down raiding Hanover and all, except Cromb, were killed. It is sad to think that our efforts were to some extent in vain, and it seems doubly tragic that, after going through so much, the men we rescued were to be sent back so soon to operations over Germany, this time never to return. It demonstrates just how much courage and how great a sacrifice were demanded of the crews of bomber command at that time. That winter was to be the severest yet for those men and the chances of completing their tour were heavily stacked against them. Indeed, it almost took a miracle to survive, which was exactly what our next group of survivors believed they had experienced.

CHAPTER 9

The Day Dimbleby was Dumb

'Some are born great, some achieve greatness, and many more have greatness snatched away from them.' That amendment to Shakespeare's famous line could apply to what happened to us next in that month of September 1943.

'All boats prepare for sea.' The sudden, unusual message brought over from the dockside Nissen hut which served as our flotilla office, took me by surprise. I was spending our supposed day of rest from operations catching up on admin. duties, chart corrections and all the form filling that a Jimmy the One had to deal with on our little ships, and I was planning to take one of our very attractive depth-charge maintenance Wrens to Grimsby for an evening at the cinema. So it was with some annoyance that I called the quartermaster to the wheelhouse to take the command across to Andy, who was at a pre-lunch gin session on 520. I then watched him making his way towards the dock gates to collect our orders from the naval base, whilst his puzzled fellow COs emerged from 520's wardroom hatch to clamber back to their own commands. Fortunately our Wrens were working on the boats, so cancelling the date presented no problem and there was still time for my opposite number, Roy Marshall, from 553, to join me for a quick tot and an attempt to find a reason for the unexpected summons. But our discussion had made little headway before a further message arrived requiring us to prepare to accommodate a couple of passengers each from the senior staff at the base.

The mystery deepened when Andy arrived back for lunch and proved quite uncommunicative on the matter, except to say that we should all be leaving the lock on the afternoon tide and heading for a given position well out to the North-East of the Humber. In addition, I had to rush around, making doubly sure that we were well provisioned for our extra guests, that everything was absolutely spotless and shipshape, guns and ammunition at the ready, sick bay, blankets, medicines all in order. It seemed as if we were to be ready for inspection by royalty.

In the early afternoon, our guests from the ops room began arriving at the dockside, expecting to be distributed aboard the boats and bedded down for the trip. There was the base Commander, the Senior Officer Ops, the Signals Officer, Guns, even 'Waste', the waste disposal officer, whose only function, as far as we knew, was to supervise the emptying of the gash-bins. He certainly knew how to empty our bottles of Scotch and gin. We were fortunate in having only the senior medical officer, who was a very nice chap from Tyneside. But what, we wondered, had made these shore-based types so keen all of a sudden to taste salt water? They were frequent visitors when the gin pennant was flying, but they had never

before shown any inclination to linger when sailing orders arrived and we had to make ready
for sea. The mystery was tantalising.

When all our guests had been found a berth, and our hasty preparations were complete, we
sailed in line astern down the Humber to Grimsby, where we, as leader, found an RAF tender
waiting to present us with yet another passenger. This time I was amazed to see the bulky
figure of none other than Richard Dimbleby haul himself over the ship's side, accompanied
by a BBC engineer and a mountain of recording equipment. This was the man who had
flown with the bombers to Berlin. He didn't waste his time on the everyday routines of
wartime. Something big was coming our way! But what? Andy was still silent on the
purpose of our mission. One thing, however, was certain: this wasn't a normal search
operation.

With our little 2-bunk wardrooms given over to our visitors and all their gear, we headed
out through the gap in the East coast minefield and I laid on a course North-East towards a
position we had been given in the middle of the North Sea opposite the coast of Denmark.
As soon as we had left the shelter of the river and started to feel the gentle rise and fall of the
waves, in a not very heavy sea, Richard Dimbleby began to wander rather restlessly about
the narrow deck. He didn't seem to want to stay with us on the bridge, or to relax in the
wardroom, and he refused all our well-meant offers of hot cocoa and corned beef sandwiches
and baked potatoes. With darkness falling and the night air growing chilly, Andy and I
wondered how we were going to make him comfortable.

No, he didn't want to go below. He would rather not have a rest in the Sick Bay. Yes, a
duffel-coat (extra-large size) would be welcome. But no, nothing to eat, thank you.

We cast anxious glances at his silent, shadowy figure as he gloomily supported himself on
the only form of seating available: one of the steel ammunition lockers for the oerlikon,
distinctly uncomfortable with its projecting locking handles. Where was he going to sleep, if
he still refused to use our wardroom? At last he solved for himself the problem of finding a
resting place. Just aft of the wheelhouse and bridge, stowed alongside the funnel on the port
side, we carried a 15 ft drop-keel, lugsail dinghy, which was covered with a canvas awning
to prevent it from filling with the water which cascaded in torrents over the bridge in rough
weather. Hoisting himself on to this, he created for himself a kind of hammock as the canvas
cover, secured by lashings around the keel, sagged beneath his weight. We gave him a pillow
and covered him with blankets, and there he remained, silent, motionless, rocked literally in
the cradle of the deep, as we sailed on over the dark and lonely sea.

When I judged that we had reached our designated position, we all cut engines and lay to,
keeping radio silence and waiting for further orders. There was a chilly breeze and a slight
swell, which changed the motion of the boat to a slow roll from side to side, accompanied by
the splash of the waves and the regular clonk, clank of objects in the ship's lockers – chains,
buckets, ammunition boxes and so on. The engineer delightedly went around collecting
recordings of sound effects for future use. But the rounded form on the dinghy lay still,
heedless of our chatter as the crew spent the night watches moaning about the way we were
kept at sea, idle and uncomfortable, and forgotten by those in charge, back on shore.

'What's he here for sir?'

'He won't be much bleeding good if it comes to reporting on anything.'

'What's he going to have to report on? Ain't nothing happened yet, nor likely to happen if
that lot on shore mucks us about like they usually do.'

'Messed me about proper. I was getting on all right, got me feet under the table. I
promised her I'd be there by eight o'clock for supper. She won't believe me when I tell her
we was sent out here to hang about doing nothing.'

I turned around at one point, to see the dark form of the engineer, with microphone in hand, recording for his future amusement the bitter comments on our situation, liberally sprinkled, as was usual in wartime, with quantities of unrepeatable expletives. Do his discs still survive on some dusty shelf at the BBC, I wonder?

The hours went by. The great man neither moved nor spoke. Dawn broke over a dark and peaceful sea. Still we waited and wondered and there was no signal from the base. All night and all day we continued to roll gently on a smooth and empty sea, until eventually, as darkness closed in once more, the signal came that we were to return, empty-handed.

Nothing had happened. No ship or aircraft had appeared. There had been no sudden call to action, in fact nothing exciting at all for Britain's ace reporter to record! All night and all day he had scarcely stirred, saying nothing, eating nothing. My personal concern now was to maintain our reputation in front of this distinguished company of senior officers. Would my navigation stand the test? Much to my relief, several hours later, dead ahead and dead on time, we sighted on the dark horizon the tiny winking light of the buoy we were aiming for, which marked the convoy route that led us back to the Humber. As soon as we had passed through the boom and were in the calm water of the river, the recumbent figure stirred, came to life and joined us on the bridge, where he made a souvenir recording of our cheerful songs as the lights of home gleamed over the murky water.

Andy has the recording still. There are long drawn out choruses of 'She's an old-fashioned lady, with old-fashioned ways' from our sentimental cockney contingent, a rendering of 'Blaydon Races' from the Medical Officer, and my own contribution of my native anthem, 'Widecombe Fair' in a variety of keys. Not quite what he had expected to be recording when he joined us.

At Grimsby the great man thankfully returned to solid land, and a few hours later our guests wound their unsteady way back to their quarters in the base, after consuming the last of our supply of duty-free spirits.

Now, long, long afterwards, the mystery has been cleared up. Andy has revealed what happened when he reported to Staff Officer Ops. This is his version of the event:

'You've been chosen for a very special mission, Andrews,' said the SOO. 'If it is successful, you can expect there will be recognition in some form. Here are your sealed orders, not to be opened until you are at sea. You will be in command of the operation, although I and a number of senior officers from the base will accompany you. You will accommodate the Senior Medical Officer in case there are casualties needing attention. The others will be distributed among your flotilla. You'll also be taking on board Richard Dimbleby and his engineer: they'll join you off Grimsby. I'll send a sailing signal shortly. Don't forget, secrecy is the of the utmost importance.'

I reeled away in a bit of a daze and returned to my wardroom for a thoughtful drink.

'What's it all about?' I wondered. Secret mission, with a chance of recognition, and with Richard Dimbleby aboard? Perhaps we are going to raid a German Radio station, and Richard Dimbleby will give a blow by blow commentary. But no one could imagine Waste and co. taking part in anything like that. Anyway, the first thing was to check that we were fully ready for sea, with fuel, food and ammunition. Then the skippers of the rest of the flotilla had to be warned to be fully prepared, with no inkling, however, of what it was all about. The off-duty boats might have sent men ashore for provisions or on compassionate leave, so these would have to be covered by temporary drafts from the base. All this checking sent all kinds of buzzes round the flotilla: the imagination that every sailor can bring to bear on a given situation is beyond belief!

Then it all started. The various senior officers came aboard, a sailing signal arrived by hand, and we were off, out through the lock and on to Grimsby, where every eye opened wide, as Richard Dimbleby and his engineer clambered aboard, giving rise to even more vivid rumours concerning our mission.

As soon as we reached the open sea, I retired to the wardroom, to be alone when I opened and read my sealed orders. These told me to proceed to a given point in the North Sea, within reach of the Danish coast, and to rendez-vous with Danish fishing boats bringing the Danish royal family and court. We were to take them on board and carry them back to Britain. Other details related to radio signals, radio silence and emergency procedures.

My first thought was that we had no Danish royal flag to hoist when the royal party stepped aboard! The second was: could we make one up, from a tablecloth perhaps? The third was: where could we find the royal insignia, anyway? Was it in the Nautical Almanac? Then more immediate concerns demanded attention, the word was passed to the other skippers in the flotilla and we set course for the rendez-vous.

Soon Richard Dimbleby began to cause us concern. The sea was calm, but MLs always had a slight movement which could make anyone uneasy who was unused to them. When meals were brought to the bridge he preferred not to eat. Eventually he found himself the ideal resting place, just near enough to the uncomfortable and rather crowded bridge and amidships, where the roll and pitch would be felt least. It was on the canvas cover of the dinghy, which was kept on the casing of the engine room.

Meanwhile, we sailed on through the North Sea, keeping a watch for the fishing boats and anything more lethal that might turn up. But we were alone on an empty expanse of calm water. As dusk was falling, we reached the position we had been given. We stopped engines, keeping the crew at action stations, however, to be prepared for attack by enemy planes or surface craft.

As we waited my tired mind was occupied with a whole range of unaccustomed problems. Where were the fishing boats I had been told to expect? Were we in the right position? Was the radio working? Were we listening on the right frequency? Had the coxswain got his pipe ready to pipe the king aboard? Where was my best uniform under all the radio equipment? When should the crew be ordered to change out of their grimy seagoing gear into number ones, ready to man the side for his majesty? Where would the royal party be accommodated with the wardroom full of recording gear? I sent for Bowler, the SBA, and kept him busily polishing an already spotless sick bay, since that was the only space available.

Time went by. We still watched and waited. I read the orders again. Were we in the right place? We checked and checked again. The darkness remained unbroken. Richard Dimbleby, covered with blankets, remained unmoving in his improvised hammock. Dawn broke and still the sea was empty. The day crept slowly by, with no movement from Richard and no contact with the shore. It was late afternoon when at last the sound of morse floated up from the wireless cabin. The message said simply: "Return to base".

On our return, I learnt that the royal family's escape plan had not been carried out, so there was to be no recognition for services rendered. And I was under orders to tell no one of the purpose of our trip, for fear that it would bring about reprisals in Denmark, if the escape plan became known to the enemy.

Unknown to us at the time, there was a great upheaval going on in Denmark. After the occupation of the country, the Germans had treated the Danes quite leniently, allowing them to keep a certain amount of self-government. In August 1943, however, the people began to grow restless and there were clashes with the occupation forces which led to more repressive measures by the Germans. In September, following more disturbances, the Nazis took over complete control of the country and its government and arrested numbers of Army officers and civilians. This provoked a general uprising. The court resigned, the Danish fleet scuttled itself, there was fighting in Copenhagen and the royal family was expected to make a dash for freedom. Instead, however, the king was forced to remain, thus depriving us of the excitement and the undoubted fame which would have come our way. So that, then, was why we had all those chair-borne brass-hats on board: they were hoping to pick up the Knights Grand Crosses and other gongs which would be handed out for rescuing the Danish royals. And Dimbleby was there to give his majesty the red-carpet treatment. Andy would certainly have been loaded with honours and I might even have been noticed myself as the chap who got them there and back – perhaps.

Alas, it all came to nothing. As in the case of a former Prince of Denmark, at the end 'the rest was silence'! To this day most Danes have not heard of the attempted escape of the royal family. It all had to remain secret for fear of reprisals against all those involved in the plan. Dimbleby never reported it and, understandably enough, his son never mentioned the undignified episode in his biography.

Still, even if fame eluded us, ours must have been the only operation in which Dimbleby was silent from start to finish. Seagoing in an RML did what flying over Germany or riding through France on a tank could not accomplish – and that's an achievement in itself!

Officers of Q 69 RML Flotilla. Left to right: (Back row) Lt Smith, S. Lt Marshall, Lt Sheppard, Base Engineer, S. Lt Brown (Guns). (Front row) S. Lt Bayliss, Andy, S. Lt Barton, Author.

CHAPTER 10

Friendly Fire

In spite of the occasional air raid, which usually concentrated on Hull, rather than Immingham, we had further proof that we were in more danger from our own side than from our enemies when we came back from leave, after a refit at J.S. Doig's, the Grimsby Yard where 547 had been built in 1942.

Our gleaming camouflage paint and our new power-operated 2-pounder pom-pom gun, which had replaced the twin .5 turret, made us the envy of the other boats as we joined them at the 'trot', after fuelling at the petrol barge.

Bill Snell, our admin. officer, greeted us cordially when we went to his dockside office to see about returning to the duty rota.

'There's a special job for you tomorrow,' he said. '520 and 550 are on call and 553 needs to service the engines, so you won't mind doing this. They need a boat to do some target towing at the DEMS firing range up the coast. They train Merchant Navy gunners up there. There's nothing to it: just running up and down a few cables off shore for an hour or so. You pick up the target in Hull at 0900.'

The weather was fine, and this seemed a good way of running in the engines before resuming normal duties, so next morning we collected the target and headed out around Spurn point towards the restricted area marked on the chart as a firing range, a few miles further north.

On the way we experimented with the target, which proved an obstinate contraption. It consisted of a small raft, about 6ft by 4ft, with a vertical tube in the centre which had a wide opening at the underwater end and a spout at the top. The idea was to tow this at such a speed as to keep it on a level keel whilst forcing the water through the intake with force enough to produce a plume of spray out of the spout. This had to be high enough to give the trainee Oerlikon gunners on shore a clear enough target to aim at – and far enough astern to ensure that we were clear of danger. It was easy enough to lower it over the side by means of our small derrick, but as soon as we streamed it behind us it jinked from side to side and would only run reasonably steadily on a fairly short tow-line. At too slow a speed there was no spray; too fast, it dug its bows into the water. We began to realise the job wasn't as simple as had at first appeared.

By the time we had reached the practice area we had managed to get the target to skid along behind us under reasonable control, with just enough spray to distinguish it from the wave-crests. We exchanged signals with the shore, hoisted the towing signal and started our first run across the range. Soon a stream of tracer hose-piped towards us, skimming the water and bouncing about some distance from the delicate white plume we were trying to keep going some 10 fathoms behind us. It became apparent that we were going to have to keep our heads well down. I was reminded only too vividly of the enthusiastic but ill-judged fire of the DEMS gunners on Russian convoy, blasting off regardless as German torpedo bombers flew between the lines of ships. From his seat on the bridge, Andy nobly conned the ship, whilst I kept an eye, under as much cover as possible, on what was happening ashore and astern of us.

We completed the first run, North to South, and swept around in a wide circle to come in and begin another. This time we were running North, with our port side to the shore. Again the tracer streamed somewhat haphazardly towards the target, but not too dangerously near at first, since the angle of fire carried the rebounds away from us. It was when we had passed the centre of the range, and the tracer began to follow us at an ever narrowing angle, that things started to look nasty. It would only need a slight swing of the body by an awkward gun-aimer to turn us into the target, instead of the unsteady spray.

'It's time they ceased fire,' I said. 'Look at those ricochets! They're spinning off at an angle.'

At that moment, before we could make a signal, it happened. A shell hit the boat's wake and flew towards us. I ducked, as something whizzed over the bridge. Andy had no time to move.

'Strewth! I felt the wind of that on my cheek!' he gasped in astonishment, as the shell sped by, missing him by a whisker.

At the same moment a crash and a clatter came from the engine room. I seized the Aldis lamp and flashed the shore, whilst the coxswain struggled with the wheel as the boat ceased to answer the helm and started to swing violently round to port.

'Stop both,' shouted Andy. 'Lower the towing signal. Engine room report damage.'

Taff Williams's dazed face appeared out of the engine-room hatch.

'We've been hit,' he cried, indignantly. 'Is everyone all right up there?'

Meanwhile, through the voice-pipe, Mason, the Motor Mechanic, was reporting reassuringly that no-one was hurt and the engines were still in working order. The ship, however, was out of control, going round in a tight circle.

The firing had stopped almost immediately, so we were able to assess the damage further as the ship kept moving slowly round and round, until it came to a stop. Fortunately, no-one was hurt, but a shell had entered the engine-room, high up on the port side, piercing our thin double skin of mahogany, whizzing over the Hall-Scott engines, bouncing off various pipes and stanchions and ending up in the trunking which carried the starboard steering control to the rudder. The fuel pipes were intact and there was no serious damage to the engines, but it was impossible to steer in the normal way. We had to abandon our target-towing, haul in the target, disconnect the rudder and limp back to Grimsby, steering by means of our two engines, altering speed on each as required to move to port or starboard. What would have happened if we had been hit by an incendiary bullet in the nearby petrol tanks we dared not imagine.

Our comrades were by no means pleased to find us back in the repair yard, enjoying an extra spell ashore at their expense, but at least no-one was called on to do that job again.

However, it didn't prevent our friends in ops, from thinking up another unpleasant task for us that winter, in the intervals between the raids on Germany. It was called 'Operation Mackerel', an appropriately fishy title, as it involved doing a policing job on the Hull and Grimsby trawler fleets.

Inevitably, most of the best traditional fishing grounds were out of bounds because of the huge minefield which protected the East coast. It was also necessary to keep the coastal convoy routes free of stray vessels which might cause confusion when German E-boats were on the prowl. The trawlermen were therefore confined to very limited coastal waters, and they were naturally very frustrated, especially since they were aware that the restricted area marked on the chart, showing the East Coast mine barrage, was not actually sown with mines to its full extent. They realised that there was a generous safety allowance on the actual mined zone, and the storms of past winters had reduced the density of the minefield. Many mines had broken adrift. In fact, drifting mines were our principal danger when crossing the area in darkness and we always had to keep a sharp lookout. Whenever they were spotted, they were sunk by gunfire. Sheppard, of 550, claimed the record for sinking six mines in one day, in December 1943, but he was always a bit of a lineshooter!

The consequence was that the fishing boats had gradually edged further and further into the forbidden zone, considering the risk worth taking in order to get the fish which the country needed. Whether any of them had been blown up it is impossible to know, but they were certainly heading into danger and also were probably annoying the convoy escorts by showing up in unexpected places on their radar screens. So we were given orders to search the minefield, to identify any vessels we found, confirm that they were engaged in trawling and record their precise position, so that appropriate official action could be taken.

As darkness fell on the 12th December, accompanied by 553, we left the Humber and headed up the convoy route to 52D buoy and then due East into the minefield towards the area in which the trawlers had been reported to be operating. They were not difficult to find with lookouts posted with night glasses on the bridge and in the crow's nest, and two more, of course, scouring the sea ahead for any mines they might have disturbed.

'Light bearing red 30,' came Ainsworth's report from the masthead, soon after we had crossed the danger line.

A yellow glow could be seen, casting a faint light downwards over the deck of a black, shadowy vessel. Trawlers were permitted to use a heavily shaded lamp to give the crew enough light to work by, since they obviously could not handle the trawl in complete darkness, so they were easily spotted. It was probably this light which was responsible for some of the unsuccessful searches which resulted from reports by returning bombers of flashing lights out at sea.

Soon several more lights became visible, swaying slightly in the moderate sea. Doug Tratner, on 553, closed us and agreed to sweep around further to the eastward whilst we tackled the boats on this side of the fleet. The skipper of our first victim must have been quite surprised to hear the roar of our Hall-Scott engines, which sounded exactly like a twin-engined bomber at close quarters. And he must have been even more surprised when our searchlight beam stabbed out of the darkness and swung across his bow to light up his number, then moved aft to linger on his nameplate, which was not too easy to read without drawing very close. When it had been identified, Clem Woodhead passed the name and number on to me down in the wheelhouse, together with the confirmation that the trawl was being operated. I was soon kept busy recording in detail our rapid changes of course and speed and pin-pointing on the chart the exact position of each vessel as we closed them, one after another. The skippers very quickly realised what we were up to. Soon they started manoeuvring to get away but, working in partnership with 553, we were able to head them off or overtake them, due to our greater speed and manoeuvrability.

It was then that things began to get nasty, as they showed their annoyance by putting the helm hard over as we hove alongside, and threatening to ram us or to bring their higher and heavier bows crashing down on our frail wooden sides. We had the added danger of fouling their trawl if we didn't back off, so it was a cat and mouse game, with Andy, and also Doug on 553, having to manoeuvre very skilfully to hang on long enough to get all the information we needed, without having our bows stove in. It was very much like the 'cod wars' with Iceland many years later, and the pitch dark night and the possibility of hitting a loose mine made it all the more dangerous.

We spent most of the night searching the mined area and logging culprits, ending up with no less than sixteen of them. Next day we sent in our report, with names, numbers and positions. A week or two later, Andy was summoned to give evidence to a court in Hull, where, presumably, the skippers were fined for disobeying the wartime regulations.

Whatever the punishment was, it apparently had no effect on the trawlermen. One morning towards the end of January, we were sent out again on what was called, this time, 'Operation Sprat'. We spent the whole day searching the same area and found five trawlers on the edge of the forbidden zone and eleven well inside it, all fishing, including several of those we had reported on the previous occasion! This was obviously their preferred fishing ground and no-one was going to stop them from using it!

Meanwhile, however, we had been putting to sea in some pretty foul weather to carry out the duties we were really intended for. The 'Battle of Berlin' was still being fought, although the raids were not so frequent because of the winter weather conditions, and we had succeeded against all the odds in making a most remarkable rescue.

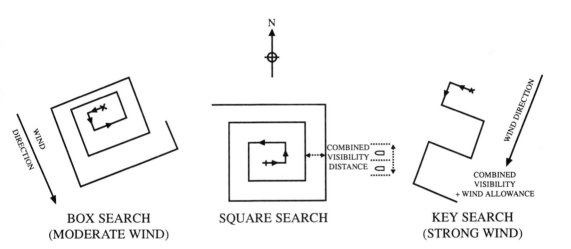

BOX SEARCH (MODERATE WIND)   SQUARE SEARCH   KEY SEARCH (STRONG WIND)

Search patterns

CHAPTER 11

Was it a Miracle?

For the crew of a bomber returning from the ordeal of a raid deep into Germany, damaged by flak or enemy fighters, the North Sea in mid-winter offered little hope of survival if the engines finally failed and they felt its icy grip. Rough seas made ditching difficult and the aircraft could break up immediately on impact; low cloud frequently prevented air search; visibility at sea level was reduced to a few yards; and the wind could carry a dinghy before it at a remarkable speed, far from its original estimated position, which might not have been very accurate in the first place. The chances of finding a tiny dinghy in such a vast area of sea, by purely visual means, in a slow speed search by a pair of small ships, were slight indeed. And survival depended too on being found before the exposure to freezing wind and water took its toll on the dinghy's occupants. Anyone plucked from the sea in those conditions might be justified in feeling that he owed his life to a miracle. But why should certain persons be selected to live when so many, equally deserving, were going to their deaths each night, and their own comrades had perhaps gone down with the aircraft? This was a question I found myself puzzling over after a particularly remarkable rescue in early 1944.

After bad weather had caused a lull in the air battle over Germany, Harris decided on another raid on the night of January 20th, which meant that in the early evening we and RML 520 were heading down river again on the familiar trip out to the Outer Dowsing waiting position. Although the buoy marking the shoal was unlit, I was pretty sure we were not too far out in our bearing and distance from the Humber light vessel when we cut engines and lay to, rolling quite heavily in a roughish sea, stirred up by a stiff northerly breeze.

'They can't be going to Berlin tonight, in this weather,' said Boswell, as we shared the middle watch on the heaving and swaying bridge.

'No, we'll be in the tram heading for Cleethorpes by seven o'clock tonight,' said Flash, who had come up for a breath of air and a cup of the kye with which we were comforting ourselves, as usual, in the cold night air. Flash was the eternal optimist, but it certainly looked as though this was going to be another of those uncomfortable and frustrating excursions: a wet, sleepless night followed by a day back in harbour, working to make everything shipshape again and catching up on chart corrections and the endless stream of signals about enemy mine-laying and new wrecks. A Number One's life was not an easy one, I reflected, as at last I was relieved by Andy and went aft to snatch a little sleep.

It was quite surprising what one grew accustomed to sleeping through in wartime conditions. In spite of being flung from side to side in my bunk, to the accompaniment of clangs and thuds from the cupboards and the thumping of waves against the hull, I drifted quickly off into an exhausted sleep, only to find myself being shaken awake a couple of hours later by Tom Goodwin.

'New orders, sir,' he said, as the engines roared into life and the ship's motion began to change to a pitching and twisting which indicated, to my surprise, that unless the wind had changed we were heading East. Surely we ought to be heading back towards the Humber, I thought.

A faint hint of dawn gave us light enough to spot the North Dowsing buoy as I gave Andy a course for the new waiting position to which we had been sent, fifty miles to the East. From then onwards it was the usual procedure of keeping a check on course and speed and ensuring a sharp lookout over the white-crested waves and the low grey clouds which scudded before an increasing northerly wind. By lunch-time we were on position, as far as I could judge by making due allowance for wind and tide, and rolling idly as we waited for fresh instructions from our tormentors at Nore HQ.

Darkness was beginning to fall before the signal came through, sending us unbelievably back to wait at the Outer Dowsing again. Midnight found us at approximately the right spot, although of course the buoy was invisible in the pitch darkness. By this time a full gale was blowing. We tried to anchor, so as not to be blown too far to the South, but the rapid rise and fall of the bow and the snatching at the slender cable of our light anchor made this impossible, and the coxswain and his helpers had a desperately difficult time hauling in and stowing the anchor again, with the waves sweeping over them on the pitching fo'c'sle. We were obliged to try to maintain our position by steaming at slow speed into the wind and then turning on the opposite course for short periods, since cutting engines was out of the question. Consequently, after having to navigate so long by dead reckoning, with no sight of a buoy and in such unfavourable weather conditions, we were not at all sure of our starting position when, at three in the morning, a signal came through ordering us to proceed to a position about 60 miles East of Flamborough Head, where an aircraft was reported to have ditched.

I laid on a course of NNE into the teeth of the gale, estimating, as well as I could, the speed that we were making in those difficult conditions. The screws were lifting out of the water as we dipped into the waves, and the boat's head was swinging, making it difficult to keep a steady course and to estimate our rate of progress. As dawn broke, RML 520 took up a position on our starboard beam so as to cover as wide a strip of water as possible, although in the heavy seas the visibility distance was minimal. As I watched 520, I would at one moment see her rise on a wave-crest, showing the long red curve of her keel as she rolled and dipped into the following trough. The next moment she would appear to have sunk almost completely beneath the surface, leaving only the tip of her mast and her ensign visible. If we were going to spot a dinghy, it would have to be virtually under our bow. But how could we expect to get so close? We had none of the modern aids to navigation. We had no echo-sounder, nothing to measure our speed or distance run. We couldn't even use a series of soundings with a lead-line, as we did on some occasions in calm weather, to check our position by matching them on the chart. I always kept a meticulous log, working out our position with careful use of the tidal information on the chart, arguing that even though I couldn't expect to be 100% accurate, rough guesswork would get us nowhere. But we had now been over twenty-four hours without a sight of a buoy, affected by wind and tide to an extent which it was difficult to judge. The dinghy, of course, would also be carried away from its original ditching position at a different relative rate to the movement of the water from our own. The actual time of ditching was unknown; there were variations in the currents in different parts of the sea; the wind would affect us both differently. It wasn't just a simple question of drawing a triangle on a chart, so as to get us from A to B by steering a course allowing for the speed and direction of the tide. With so many unknowns, it all added up to a virtually insoluble problem in navigation.

Andy and I looked carefully at the chart, discussing our best course of action. We reckoned that if we could at least confirm the accuracy of our own position we would reduce the odds against us.

'There's a direction-finding station on the coast here, near Hull,' I said, and another north of us at Cullercoats. If they could give us a fix. . .'

'Right,' said Andy, 'We'll ask for permission to transmit and get them each to give us our bearing. The angle's wide enough to be reasonably accurate. How long is it before we reach the ditching area?'

'Another three hours,' I replied, 'That should be time enough.'

The reply to our signal was reasonably prompt, fixing a time for us to transmit our call-sign, so that the two bearings could be taken. However, for some reason Cullercoats failed to obtain a bearing and only the Humber D/F station was able to respond, so that we knew only that we were somewhere on a line running North-East into the North Sea. There were obviously limits as to how far along this line, East or West, we could be, so I was able to adjust the plot to some extent, using my common-sense to bring it into line with the new information. But the hopes of finding the dinghy still seemed extremely slight, especially since, with the low cloud and high wind still persisting, there would be no search aircraft to assist us. Our best hope was that the airmen might be able to operate a hand-held transmitter. This was a small box which would transmit an SOS if its handle was turned fast enough. But it depended on an aerial usually suspended from a kite, which would be very difficult to fly in a high wind and choppy sea. Jim Cannon, with his bucket beside him, kept an uncomfortable but careful wireless watch on the frequency, in the hope of hearing a faint signal, but heard nothing.

At eleven o'clock I reckoned that we must have reached the original position of the ditching, allowing for the effects of wind and sea.

'With this wind, there seems no point in going any further to the North,' I said, 'It will have been carrying the dinghy – if there is any – pretty rapidly southwards.'

'And if we do a normal box search,' said Andy, 'we'll be wasting our time, letting it drift further and further south, while we go round in circles.'

We agreed that the only sensible thing to do was to run on an extended leg before the wind, covering a fresh ribbon of sea parallel to our previous approach, in the hope of overtaking the supposed dinghy. So we headed West for ten minutes and then turned back on a heading of SSW, with 520 coming around to starboard of us again. This very primitive down-wind search was all that was feasible in the circumstances, so it was southwards once again, with all hands keeping a sharp lookout.

'I reckon that with the wind astern an hour's run should be enough. Then we'll go East for thirty minutes and do a shorter run North again,' I suggested.

Andy agreed. 'At least we can see better for a time, without the wind and the spray in our eyes,' he added.

'If there is anybody alive out here, God help 'em,' said the coxswain, gloomily.

During all this time, unknown to us, another individual drama in the course of the air war had been unfolding. The target for the night of the 21st had been Magdeburg, instead of Berlin. At 1950, at Snaith in Yorkshire, the crew of Halifax LW 468, J for Johnny of 568 Squadron, piloted by Sergeant Hugh Melville, had set out on only their third op, to face the increasingly effective German defences. Their night-fighters came up in strength and the bomber stream was heavily attacked. Of the 648 bombers, 56 were lost, 4 of them being shot down by the famous fighter ace Prince zu Sayn Wittgenstein before he himself was shot down and killed. J for Johnny, however, reached the target unscathed and Flying-Officer Williams, the bomb-aimer, was able to report bombs gone right over the target. Feeling quite pleased with themselves, they started on the return journey. Everything seemed to be going well for them, with no sign of enemy activity. But unfortunately this was because they had somehow strayed North of the prescribed course. Suddenly they found the sky around them filled with exploding shells and Melville was forced to increase altitude to 24,000 feet and alter course to avoid the flak.

'That was a bit of a bumpy ride,' said Melville. 'Where did that lot come from?'

'Sorry, skipper,' replied Sgt Mansfield, his navigator, 'the wind seems to have carried us further north than I expected. I reckon we were over the Elbe estuary. Those were the Hamburg defences. But we're not far from the coast now.'

'Well, we seem to have got clear of that little lot all right. Give me a course for Flamborough,' said Melville, 'and keep your eyes skinned, there could still be fighters about.'

Soon they were over the North Sea, heading for home and feeling that the worst of the danger was past. But then Sgt Baldrey, the flight engineer, noticed that the fuel gauge was registering an alarming drop.

'There seems to be something wrong with the fuel supply, skipper,' he reported. 'We appear to have only four hundred gallons left in the tanks. That's barely enough to get us home.'

As they flew onwards he watched the gauge with growing anxiety. 'We're down to two hundred,' he said, only ten minutes later. 'The tanks must have been holed when we got that pasting over the Elbe.'

'There could be some left in the tanks we used on the outward trip,' said Melville. 'Try switching over.'

'No joy there,' replied the flight engineer, 'they're empty.'

'We won't make landfall if we go on losing fuel at that rate,' said the navigator. We'd better warn base that we might have to ditch.'

Whilst his comrades anxiously watched the precious fuel drain away, Sgt Godfrey, the wireless operator, got a mayday signal away, and then clamped down his key, transmitting a continuous signal, so that at least there would be an accurate fix on their position when they were forced to ditch. Then they went to ditching stations in the centre fuselage, whilst Melville remained at the controls, nursing the aircraft as far as it would go towards home.

Finally, with the fuel guages showing 'empty', Melville had to make a decision. The engines were still running, but the last few drops of fuel were needed to keep them going long enough for him to maintain control of the aircraft as they ditched.

'Hold tight,' shouted Melville, 'we're going down.'

He held the aircraft steady as they glided down towards the wind-tossed sea, making a remarkable landing, for the aircraft remained afloat. Even the perspex nose was still intact. However, getting into the dinghy in those weather conditions proved tragically difficult. The automatic release failed to function, and Sergeant Baldrey climbed out on the wing to hack at the release mechanism, whilst F/O Williams went into the icy water to help him. Although they succeeded in freeing the dinghy, its tether broke and it was swept away. They all had to swim for it. Sgt Baldrey, no doubt exhausted by his efforts, and Sgt Lester vanished in the darkness. As the others struggled to control the dinghy and clamber in, it capsized, losing most of its contents. F/O Williams, also, was suffering badly from exposure, but between them the other four managed at last to right the dinghy and get him in. Then there was nothing for it but to bale furiously and hope that with daylight help might be at hand.

Huddling down to avoid the wind and spray, they did what they could to make their frozen comrade comfortable and searched the pockets of the dinghy for the Horlicks tablets, fishing lines, marker dye and other aids which should have been there; but everything seemed to have been lost, including the vitally important hand-operated transmitter. As the chill, damp hours went by, they grew increasingly resigned to the fate which all too probably awaited them. The plane had of course been sunk by the rough seas. When daylight revealed the thick grey cloud hanging low above the water, it became obvious that there was little hope of a successful air search. They watched their exhausted comrade grow weaker and finally die, showing such calm, patient fortitude that they felt that, if rescue proved impossible, they themselves could face death with the same quiet courage.

Then, suddenly, moving his cramped body to ease the discomfort of lying in cold seawater on the unsteady fabric of the dinghy, Mansfield felt a hard object beneath his thigh. There was something in one of the pockets which they must have overlooked earlier on.

'Hey, look what I've found, chaps,' he said, as he drew out a Very's pistol and a pack of cartridges. 'There's a chance for us yet, if anything comes near enough to see a flare.'

'D'you reckon there are any search aircraft out in this weather ?' asked Godfrey.

'There could at least be some HSLs,' Melville replied. 'They got our signal and they must know roughly where we are. There must be someone out looking for us.'

'But in this wind and sea, and with visibility as low as this they won't have much chance of finding us,' said his comrade gloomily. 'Our only hope is a change in the weather before nightfall.'

Stirred by this discovery to a mixture of faint hope and contrasting despair, for some time they discussed the chances of survival. Could they really expect a search aircraft to appear in those conditions, or a ship to come near enough to find them? Would they have the strength to last out long enough? What was the best way to make use of these few precious flares? As the time crawled slowly by and the cold began to take its effect, they felt themselves slipping gradually into unconsciousness. At length, realising that their strength was ebbing fast, they came to a decision: they must take some action whilst they could. They agreed that they would fire off the cartridges at intervals. If, by some quirk of fate, anyone was near enough to see them, they could hope to be saved. If not, they would resign themselves to the inevitable, hoping that they would be able to face death with the same calm courage as their friend. It was almost noon.

'Here goes!' said Melville, as he slipped a cartridge into the pistol and fired it into the air. A red flare burst above their heads and was carried swiftly away by the wind, to fall back into the sea. . . .

Meanwhile our two boats had been running before the wind on our southward course, all eyes fixed on the sea around us for a glimpse of a yellow dinghy rising on a wave. As mid-day approached, I said to Andy, 'We've been on this course for an hour now, and we've had the wind behind us as well. Do you think we've gone far enough?'

'We'll turn East at noon and do another short leg to the North,' he replied.

I had just picked up the Aldis lamp, to signal a change of course to Dermot Barton, when a sudden cry came from the masthead lookout:

'520's turning sir. Flares to starboard!'

Only yards to starboard of RML 520, but so deeply hidden in the waves that it was as invisible to Eddie and his lookouts as 520 was to the ditched airmen, lay the dinghy for which we were searching. Seeing the flare, Eddie Smith turned to starboard and soon spotted the dinghy as it rose on a wave just ahead of him. Out went 520's boom and down the scrambling nets into the dinghy went her coxswain and two seamen. Carefully they hoisted the four exhausted, but thankful survivors on to the deck, to be rapidly cleaned up and settled in warm bunks by the SBA. Then the shrouded body of their comrade was laid gently on the quarter deck.

Elated by the amazing chance which had brought us so fortunately so close to the airmen at the very moment when they had decided to fire their flares, we headed homewards at our best speed. Late that night we arrived back at Grimsby and our survivors were rushed off to hospital.

We did not meet the airmen ourselves until a month or two later, when they came over to Immingham to thank us. They were convinced that their rescue was a miracle, but I could not reconcile this view with the thought of all the others, including friends of mine, and their own comrades, who had not been so fortunate. However, it was indeed remarkable that they should have found that one essential piece of equipment and fired it at the very moment when we were nearest and yet about to head away from them. Was it chance that brought us together and guided our actions at that crucial moment on that vast, storm-swept sea? Could it have depended at least a little on a certain amount of experience and navigational skill on our part?

I often wondered afterwards whether that 'miracle' had justified itself by allowing those men to survive the war. I had the answer on January 21st, 1991, the 47th anniversary of the event, as the result of an article about the rescue in the Bomber Command Association's Newsletter. It took the form of a letter from Hugh Melville himself. He told me that they had indeed all survived and gone on to gain promotion and decorations for gallantry, although not all were now still alive. The news made all the more poignant the fate of the survivors of our previous rescue.

Mansfield and Melville (2nd and 3rd from left) with their re-constituted crew on their 20th mission

CHAPTER 12

Blind Man's Buff

All the modern aids to navigation, the satellite position finders carried by even small yachts and the ship to shore radios, the computers and automatic logs, make our equipment seem primitive in the extreme, yet I doubt whether one rescue, carried out by Doug Tratner and Roy Marshall in 553, could have been performed any more efficiently using the most sophisticated technology. It showed how varied the circumstances could be in which a search had to be made and how important any one of the many different items carried in a dinghy's emergency pack could be. In this case it was the simple whistle, which all airmen were later obliged to wear attached to their lapels, probably wondering what use it could possibly be. On this occasion it saved ten lives.

Before either Andy or I had been posted to 547, its skipper, Mick Innes, had been the first to bring survivors in to Immingham, when he had rescued the crew of a fishing boat in distress. But this later rescue had made 553 the first boat in the flotilla to have carried out a successful Air-Sea Rescue from a ditched aircraft.

It followed a raid on Wilhelmshaven by a squadron of Flying Fortresses on May 20th, 1943. After bombs had been released on target at 26,000ft, one of the aircraft was hit by a burst of flak under the wing, which appeared to damage both port engines. Losing speed, the Fortress dropped behind and below its formation and was immediately pounced on by the German fighters.

The Americans put up a long and gallant fight as they headed seawards, hitting back at the fighters, which attacked in relays for three hours, with fresh waves coming in constantly, determined to finish them off. Soon number four engine was hit by a burst of cannon fire; then the cowling of number two engine was blown away and a fire started. At 17,000ft the oxygen system and the intercom failed. By now there were several holes through the nose, many more through each wing, flak holes in the bomb-bay doors and cannon-shell holes along the fuselage, right up to the tail gun compartment, which had a large hole blown in it. The port elevator was badly damaged, they were losing height at 300ft per minute, and it was evident that the aircraft would not be able to reach friendly shores.

The crew had to decide whether to turn back and bale out over land, or to ditch and hope for rescue, although, since the radio and IFF had been blown to pieces, they could not send out a mayday signal. With enormous courage, they chose the hazard of ditching rather than be taken prisoner.

Fortunately, the sea was calm, there was little wind and the visibility was excellent. Systematically they prepared for ditching. They jettisoned all the guns and ammunition, with the exception of those in the top turret, and went to ditching stations. Eight of the crew, who had all miraculously survived, wedged themselves in the radio cabin, whilst the pilot and co-pilot remained at the controls.

But the Luftwaffe had not given up the chase. When they were at a height of only 350ft, another fighter swooped in to the attack. After it had swept over them, the co-pilot climbed into the top turret and waited for it to strike again. Back came the enemy pilot, confident in his belief that he was finishing off a defenceless cripple. But the American, holding his fire until the enemy was at point blank range, emptied his guns into the belly of the fighter, sending it crashing into the sea. That made the eleventh fighter claimed by the Fortress that day.

The co-pilot then returned to his seat and strapped himself in. On their one remaining engine, the pilot skilfully brought the plane down the few remaining feet, throttling back as they hit the water. The aircraft touched down on the sea, slightly tail-down, at 95 mph. The crew, in three lines, braced against the bulkhead and two sides of the radio cabin, felt the shock as the tail touched and the rapid deceleration as the aircraft ploughed along the surface of the sea. Then it came to rest, floating with about three feet of the trailing edge of the wings covered with water.

Two of the crew were knocked unconscious by a crank handle which flew off the bulkhead as they hit the sea, but the surge of water through the floor revived them. This was obviously a well-disciplined crew. They were not only well trained in the defence of their aircraft, but they had conscientiously practised their dinghy drill prior to every mission. They got quietly out, in their appointed order, through the radio hatch, each man carrying the equipment he had been detailed to bring with him. They had to break open the doors of the dinghy compartment, but soon had the dinghies out. These inflated automatically and the crew were able to climb in.

The next emergency arose when they could not release the painter of the starboard dinghy, but the pilot had a knife with which he was able to cut it free. They paddled clear of the aircraft and, three minutes later, the tail went up in the air and she gently sank.

All were wet to some extent, and the sun was not hot enough to dry their clothing, although they partially stripped and rubbed down. As night came on, they began to shiver and the waves breaking over the dinghies made them wetter still. Another such night might well be too much for some of them. They could only keep warm by cranking the dinghy radio or rowing with the paddles.

When daylight came, there was a dense fog which condensed on their clothing, and ice began to form on the hair and in the eyebrows of them all. This condition persisted throughout the day. Fortunately, however, they had two spare, small 'K' type dinghies attached to the two larger ones; so they cut the hoods and aprons from these and used them as head covers. Then they huddled together to keep warm.

Thanks to their careful dinghy drill, they had emergency rations, chocolate and water, which they shared out at regular intervals. They also had a flare pistol, and twelve parachute flares, four cans of fluorescent powder, to colour the sea around them and make themselves more conspicuous, and, most important of all, the emergency radio and its ancillary equipment.

The latter was a small yellow box with a handle on one side. By holding it between the knees and turning the handle as quickly and steadily as possible, enough power could be generated to transmit an automatic SOS signal on the 500kc international distress frequency. The aerial was a length of wire sent as high as possible, usually by means of a kite. These Americans, however, had a hydrogen balloon, which was much easier to launch. In the calm conditions they were able to inflate it enough to send it up to 150ft. For five minutes every hour and half hour, and as often as they could manage in between, they cranked away at the handle, hoping their transmissions would be heard.

By a stroke of luck, about midnight on the first night, an aircraft, which they thought was possibly a Wellington, passed overhead at about 1,000ft. In their excitement, they grabbed at the flare pistol and fumbled with the cartridge, almost failing to fire it off in time. The aircraft was, in fact, already going away from them when the flare went up, but this meant that the rear gunner spotted it. The plane returned and circled them, as they sent up another flare and made an SOS on the transmitter lamp.

The aircraft circled twice more, flashing a signal which they were unable to read, and then continued on its course. Relieved as they were by this, their hopes would have been even higher if they had known that the aircraft had actually been able to take a 'Gee' fix on their position and pass it on to Headquarters. The shore stations were alerted and they concentrated on picking up transmissions from the dinghy radio, whilst a search operation was set in motion. The crew were particularly lucky to have been spotted before the thick sea fog descended as, when day came, an air search was quite impossible. All would depend on RML 553, which was heading towards them from its patrol position and, eventually, homing on the signals with the direction-finding aerial housed in the dome on its wheelhouse roof.

A North Sea fog can be a dense, frustrating thing. Although it may only cover the surface of the sea to a height of 30 feet or so, it is so thick at sea level that one seems to be staring from the bridge into a blank screen, unable to see even the for'ard gun, only a few feet away, As time goes by, the tired eye starts to play strange tricks: I remember once thinking I could see an entire shoreline, with cranes and tall buildings, even though we were far from land. By mid-morning, Doug Tratner knew he was close to the dinghy, although, with lookouts posted all round the ship from bow to stern, nothing could be seen. The bearings from the D/F aerial kept shifting as they moved slowly to and fro, trying to pin-point the source of the transmissions, which were unfortunately intermittent and tended to fade at crucial moments as tired hands rested from the labour of cranking the handle.

What happened next had some of the ingredients of farce. Our boats' Hall-Scott aero engines made us sound like aircraft, so the Americans did not realise that what they heard through the fog was a rescue launch. They thought it was an aircraft flying towards them or away as the sound grew louder or fainter. As the sound increased, they would send up a flare in the hope of its being seen above the fog bank. This happened several times during the day, until Doug, by happy chance, saw an old life-buoy and, probably out of frustration, fired three bursts at it from the Lewis gun. With hindsight, it might have been an idea, much earlier, to have stopped engines and shouted to them through the loud hailer on the masthead. However, the firing did the trick. Hearing it, the Americans realised a ship was near and began to blow on their whistles. With ears strained to detect the direction of the sound, Doug moved slowly forward, turning to port and starboard, edging gradually towards the dinghy until, suddenly, there it was virtually under the flare of the bow.

Then it was the usual drill of hauling the dinghies alongside and cramming the ten chilled and weary men into warm, dry bunks in the wardroom and sick bay, giving them hot drinks and letting them sink into refreshing sleep. The final stages of the search had lasted into the late afternoon!

Without the careful dinghy drill, the complete equipment in good condition – flares, radio, balloon aerial, adequate rations and, ultimately, those simple whistles – those ten men could have suffered lingering deaths from cold and hunger. They were in the heart of the North Sea, a hundred miles or more from the coast of Yorkshire, and no one had been aware originally of their ditching. Here again chance had played a significant part in their rescue, combined with careful attention to detail. There was a certain amount of fatalism among aircrew which made them careless about dinghy drill and life-saving equipment, which required a lot of propaganda to overcome. I often wondered whether more lives might have been saved if more attention had been paid to quite simple details, any of which might have been the means of surviving the hazards of the sea.

CHAPTER 13

The Dunkers' Club

A bulky figure clambered clumsily out of 550's wardroom hatch and stood swaying on the quarter-deck. Then, assisted tactfully by the quartermaster on watch, it made its way unsteadily to the gangway and slumped down the mediterranean ladder clamped to the ship's side, to land heavily on the floating wooden walkway which led towards the side of the dock. Peering through the darkness, the quartermaster anxiously followed the other's movements.

'I wouldn't go that way, sir,' he called respectfully, as the departing visitor steadied himself and then turned towards the stern of the boat.

'Nonshense, I know where I'm goin',' came the garbled reply, as the somewhat inebriated officer continued to stagger towards the stern instead of the bow.

'Not that way, sir!'

The warning went unheeded.

'Sir! Look out!'

Splash!

'Man Overboard!' shouted the quartermaster, leaping down the ladder to help the surprised and struggling visitor, floundering in the thick black oily water of the dock basin, whilst Mac came tearing from the wardroom to his aid. Between them they hauled the heavy, dripping body back on to the cat walk and manouevred it, with considerable difficulty and the help of his crew, back to his own ship for a clean-up and a dry-out.

This particular character was the skipper of one of the Yarmouth MLs which, with the Lowestoft boats, used to escort coastal convoys North to the Humber and then call in at Immingham before joining the next southbound convoy. Mac and I chortled frequently over the memory of this incident, a fitting revenge for the annoyance he caused us. He had the irritating habit, as soon as he had moored alongside, whatever the time of day or night, of inviting himself aboard the nearest boat. Whoever was duty officer would groan in agony at the sound of his booming voice and the thud of his boots as he came down the companion, but it was impossible to refuse hospitality. We would then have to sit in boredom, listening to his rambling conversation well into the night, until he had drunk his fill of our ration of Scotch and decided at last to leave us in peace.

Our boats were moored in groups of two or three, bows on to the dockside. The inside boat had its ropes passed through iron rings embedded in 'dolphins', or concrete pillars, going out at a right angle into the basin. Between each two rows of dolphins a number of floating wooden 'cats', or catamarans, were secured, to enable us to walk ashore. On this occasion, our unwanted guest, who naturally must be nameless, had chosen to turn the wrong way and walk straight into the water, which contained all kinds of nauseous effluent from the vessels in the dock. Unfortunately, he wasn't the only victim of this arrangement, since there were missing cats in a number of places, particularly where the gangway narrowed towards the wooden steps up to the bank. A careless step on a dark night could result in a sudden ducking for even the least inebriated amongst us.

We had a very friendly relationship with the officers of the American Army Transportation Corps, who supervised the docking and unloading of the Liberty ships which came to Immingham. They used to be very welcome at our parties and would repay our hospitality by providing us with delicacies brought in by their ships. Some of them, too, became victims of the blackout and the missing cats, so that they suggested we form a 'Dunkers' Club', after the American term for their habit of dipping, or dunking, doughnuts in coffee.

I myself had the honour of becoming a member of the club one dark night. I was duty officer, everyone else being at sea or ashore, and sitting peacefully in our wardroom, when Flash, who was on watch on deck, suddenly called down that an ML had arrived unexpectedly and was heading for the fuelling barge. She had almost reached the inner end of the basin where the barge was moored, and it was our duty to provide hands to receive her lines. So, calling for the duty watch to follow me, I leapt over the side and went haring towards the steps. Suddenly I found myself treading not on solid wood, but filthy water, with my hat floating gently away on the ripples my plunge had caused. I think the ML must have moored safely at the barge, but I was no longer interested. Good old Flash helped me back to the boat and took my drenched clothes away to get them cleaned. For some reason I was wearing my number one doeskin suit, which took some cleaning. Flash, however, managed it as usual, with the aid of our fire extinguisher fluid – an excellent cleaning material – presenting it to me a day or two later, with his usual toothy grin, cleaned and pressed and almost like new.

We in the 69th Flotilla were a comparatively sober bunch, since half of our officers were married and had their wives in the village nearby. We had, however, some very odd characters visiting us from the convoy MLs. I remember a pair of mad Australians who drank our scotch, neat, by the tumblerful; one of them once caused a panic by suddenly whipping out a pistol and firing it wildly in the crowded wardroom – only blanks, of course, but even so the wads flew around with frightening force.

In complete contrast, our berth was shared at times by a group of converted Camper and Nicholson gunboats, flying the Red Ensign to indicate that they were merchantmen. They had names such as *Nonsuch*, *Gay Viking*, *Gay Corsair*, *Hopewell* and *Master Standfast*. With their sleek lines and powerful Paxman Diesels, they were not only good seaboats but extremely fast compared with the MLs which they superficially resembled. In the place of the normal armament and ammunition they had holds for merchandise.

Although we made efforts to be friendly, the crews carefully avoided us, giving us no indication of their purpose. The boats would disappear singly or in pairs and return many days later, often with severe damage from contact with the enemy. We realised that they had some dangerous secret mission, but we never discovered what it was. No reports of their operations ever appeared in the press. Their story has, however, since been told in *The Blockade Busters* by Ralph Barker. They were blockade runners, slipping through the Kattegat to bring vital cargoes of ball-bearings back from Sweden, or carrying secret agents, and they suffered severe casualties in the course of their activities. A number were sunk by enemy planes and patrol boats.

It must have been a grim existence, facing constant danger and never being able to relax in the normal way when they were in harbour. We had a large Nissen hut on the dockside which we cleaned up and used for recreation in various ways, organising dances to which wives, Wrens and members of the local ATS were invited, and setting up an indoor shooting range for matches with the Wrens. We also had regular games of mixed hockey on a pitch attached to the base. But those chaps were never able to join in.

Andy had reason to regret his own willingness to play hockey that winter. The Wrens, of course, were able to run rings around us with their skill in handling their sticks, and we were only able to make wild swipes at the ball. One such wild swing, from our coxswain if I remember correctly, caught Andy, who was standing too close behind him, a resounding blow in the mouth. As a result, he eventually lost four front teeth.

The climax of the Christmas festivities of that winter of 1943 was a fancy dress ball at the base, to which Andy went dressed as Hitler. He managed to get out of the dock without attracting any attention but, when he tried to return, he was stopped and put under arrest. It was not long since the mysterious arrival of Hess in Scotland, so the dock police, believing anything was possible, thought they had made the catch of the century. However, a packet or two of cigarettes and the obviously makeshift nature of his uniform soon persuaded them that he was not what he appeared to be. Apparently it didn't occur to them that Hitler couldn't possibly have been able to speak normal navy-style English!

With the coming of the new year big changes set in. The boats went off in turn for refits, resulting in the addition of more armament and equipment. We all now had power-operated pom-poms, plus rocket guns on each side of the wheelhouse. These could fire star shell as well as high-explosive shells. We had the new VHF radio, set to fixed frequencies which gave instant communication with all types of search aircraft. This would mean eventually that we would be able to talk directly to the P-47 Thunderbolts and Vickers Warwicks, which were about to be introduced to co-ordinate the Air-Sea Rescue services. The Thunderbolt fighters would carry out low-level sweeps over the southern part of the North Sea, while a Warwick, an enlarged version of the Wellington, carrying an airborne lifeboat, would keep in touch with both the searchers and returning bombers and direct us immediately to the scene of a ditching.

The biggest change, however, was our transfer from Immingham to the South coast. At the end of April the orders came through for our move to Dartmouth. This was great news for me, since it meant returning to my native Devon, but still I began to feel a tinge of regret at leaving. Immingham was a grimy, ugly place, and Grimsby, with its permanent smell of rotting fish from the glue factory, its rows of warehouses and the Ticklers jam factory, the sight of which would have put you off jam for evermore, had no attraction in itself. Cleethorpes, when the tide was in, was only a little better. It had at least a promenade and a pier of sorts, where dances were held. But we still managed to have a lot of fun there. It was always with a sense of expectation that we boarded the 'Clickety', the single-decked electric tram which ran from the dock to the iron bridge in the centre of the town. The Ship Hotel had been one of my favourite ports of call, where you could get an excellent, civilised meal for five shillings. It was an ideal place to entertain one of the charming Wrens or ATS who helped to give the town a more attractive appearance. The officers' club had always been a lively, cheerful place, with regular dances, and we were going to miss the friends we had made there. We were going to miss our friends in the base, too, but, as it turned out, I was pleased to find that one particular maintenance Wren was aiming to follow us to Dartmouth.

Whilst we were at Immingham, the flotilla had rescued 48 men in 10 successful rescue operations, for six of which 547 had been responsible. Now the Battle of Berlin had petered out and the attack was due to be switched to the Channel. D-day had been fixed and 'Overlord' was on its way. This compliment from Air Commodore John Searby, in his book *The Bomber Battle for Berlin*, makes a fitting conclusion to the account of our stay on Humberside:

We had great faith in the launch crews of the Air Sea Rescue Service. Once a position had been given – even a very approximate 'fix' – the launches went out regardless of weather or distance in an effort to pull our men from the sea, and I take this opportunity to record our admiration for a 'silent Service' which received little or no publicity yet made a valuable contribution to our safety.

After a round of farewell parties, which drained us dry of all our stocks of spirits and beer, we sailed at last, on May 10th, with pennants flying, leaving the entrance dock for the last time. All the base staff were there, the Admiral included, to wave us goodbye, just as they had been to see us safely back the year before. Then it was out to the swept channel to join a southbound convoy as temporary escort. It was quite a large convoy, with some very strange objects towed by pairs of tugs. They were huge rectangular concrete structures, large caissons, the size of three or four houses. We accompanied them around the North Foreland and as far as Dover, where we were due to fuel and spend a night. It was a beautiful, sunny day and they must have been clearly visible to the watchers across the Channel, yet they attracted no attention in the way of gunfire and presumably gave them no clue about future operations. They were to be used in fact in the Normandy invasion, to be sunk so as to form the 'Mulberry' harbour off Arromanches.

We were met with typical Coastal Force hospitality in the Dover boat pens and had an enjoyable night, despite the odd shell to remind us how near we were to France. The next two days, as we sailed down the channel, with an overnight stop at 'Hornet', the Portsmouth Coastal Force base, were like a holiday cruise in peacetime. The sea was calm, the sun shone, nothing disturbed the tranquil scene.

At Dartmouth, however, there were plenty of signs of preparations for war. Flotillas of torpedo and gun boats, including the new large, fast 'D' class, lay alongside the depot ships in mid stream and moored to the quays on the Kingswear side of the river. Landing craft of various sizes were moving up and down the river and filling every creek and inlet. There were minelaying MLs, minesweepers, water carriers and ammunition barges lining the banks and moored to lines of buoys. No one was allowed to enter or leave a forbidden zone of ten miles from the coast. We realised why we had been sent here and how soon the invasion could be expected. But where was still a mystery.

Our own berth was at a buoy out in the river between Dartmouth and Kingswear, so that we could get ashore quickly in either direction via the boats which kept up a regular service around the 'trots' and depot ships. While we waited and prepared for the great day, there was plenty of pleasure to be had on shore. The Wrens organised dances with vast quantities of Devonshire cream and fresh strawberries. We were sent around to Torquay to do guard duty at the entrance to an anti-submarine boom stretching across Torbay, where larger ships were gathered at anchor, and spent three days out of four lying at leisure at the East jetty in Torquay harbour. From there we enjoyed the freedom of the town and of the Imperial Hotel, empty of civilian visitors because of the security measures. Every day we ate delicious fresh lobster, fished up by the crew of the ack-ack gun at the end of the jetty. Normally they had nothing else to do but lie in the sun and fish, although they were taken by surprise one night, when a solitary raider swooped low right over us and dropped its bombs on the town, just beyond the harbour. Unfortunately they fell on an old people's retirement home, causing a number of casualties. It was sad that this should have been the only damage inflicted on the area as we prepared for the coming showdown. The few mine-laying aircraft which approached the coast only served to emphasise the change which had taken place since the heavy raids of 1941.

Apart from these incidents, the whole of the month of May seemed to be a period of endless sunshine, with a holiday spirit affecting everyone. It was one of those coincidences, not unusual in wartime, when things were really hotting up and yet the everyday pattern of existence could not have been more peaceful. With most of the air activity going on further up the Channel, we were unaccustomedly idle. This was just the time, of course, for the Admiralty to decide to give us the help of a third officer. I now had yet more leisure than I had been accustomed to, but I did rather enjoy having a junior to order around. Midshipman Cherry proved to be a very pleasant, capable young man, with the great asset of a sister in the Wrens on shore. His presence ensured invitations to all their social activities, providing such a variety of interest that, alas, the tentative romance which had been continued from Immingham came sadly to an end.

Meanwhile, at the end of May, we received our thick package of orders, with instructions not to open it until the moment came. We painted the universal recognition sign on the roof of the wheelhouse, a large white five-pointed star on a blue background, and waited.

The first stand-by was cancelled but, with the change in the weather, on June 4th, the signal went out to open our sealed orders, and the flotilla officers gathered in the wardroom to find out what our part was to be. To our disappointment, we were not to put to sea until D-day plus three, to take our turn in providing air-sea rescue support in the invasion area. The following day, however, from the mouth of the river Dart, we had a grandstand view of the most amazing parade of shipping that is likely ever to be seen. An endless stream of landing craft came out, in perfect order, from every nook and cranny of the river and estuary. It seemed impossible for so many to have been hidden there. Once clear of the shoreline, they slipped into place in the procession of larger ships coming slowly from the westward. We watched in amazement as, throughout the evening, for hour after hour, ships of all sizes sailed smoothly and majestically by, each in its appointed place, heading for the junction in mid Channel where the streams from East and West would converge and turn on to the routes which would lead them to the next morning's landings on the various invasion beaches.

Everyone was jubilant next day to learn of the success of the landings, but for us they proved too successful. It was decided that our services were not required, after all! We had to be content with being sent on just one or two searches, which repeated some of the problems of earlier days. During one search we saw a B-24 Liberator circling a RAF HSL, but in spite of our VHF radio, we could not get in contact. Eventually we found an empty airborne lifeboat and had to conclude that the occupants had been taken off it by the HSL. So one empty lifeboat towed back to harbour was all we had to show for our efforts whilst at Dartmouth.

Eddie Smith, on 520, was the only skipper able to shoot a line of sorts. He was sent down to the Channel Islands in the course of a search and found himself enveloped in a thick fog. He swore that when it suddenly lifted he found himself so close to Guernsey that he could read the time by the church clock. He beat a hasty retreat as the shore batteries opened up on him, making smoke from the smoke canisters that we carried at the stern.

One other consequence of our stay was a transformation in Andy's appearance. All the officers had agreed to grow a full set – of whiskers – at some well-oiled point in a pre-invasion party. They had vowed to retain them until victory was complete. However, all except Andy gradually went back on their oaths. He alone was left with a very full and fine moustache and beard, which he – and his wife Jay – found such an improvement on his former clean-shaven appearance that he kept it, not just for the duration, but right up to the present day. As it gradually became more grizzled, it made him look like the original ancient mariner. With his naturally twinkling eyes beaming through the hairy mass, he looked so impressive, in fact, that when we were visited by an American Press reporter, his photograph was specially taken to grace the cover of an issue of Time Magazine. Andy was immensely proud to be chosen as the epitome of the old English sea-dog.

Fortunately we were not allowed to stay too long in guilt-ridden idleness. The beginning of July brought orders to move back into the North Sea, to *HMS Beehive*, the very active

Coastal Force base at Felixstowe. The voyage was a repeat of our earlier one: a calm sea, summer sunshine, and stops at Portsmouth and Dover. Things were rather more hectic at Dover, however, as the V1 buzz-bombs were being sent over thick and fast. We had just been taken by our hosts to a dance on the Western docks when the evening's attack started. The whole of the ack-ack defences put up a continuous barrage, and it seemed as if Jerry was sending over shells as well. Accustomed as I had grown in the past to air raids, I didn't at all enjoy the jeep ride back to the shelter of the concrete pens. Visually the searchlights, the blazing engines of the buzz-bombs and the exploding shells were quite spectacular, but far too many buzz-bombs were being hit and falling on Dover. I wasn't sorry to leave next day for Felixstowe.

It was on July 10th that we sailed into the little harbour, tucked away behind what was then a quiet little seaside town. A flour silo was then the only sign of commercial activity, and it was beside this that we had our berth. The quay and warehouse sheds on the opposite side of the dock formed the base for the MTBs and MGBs which had earned for *HMS Beehive* a great reputation. It was perhaps the most active base in the war of the narrow seas between our 'little ships' and the German E-Boats. It was from here that Robert Hichens, one of the best known heroes of Coastal Forces had gone out to fight and inevitably, at last, to die.

On a calm, moonlit night, these boats would make a stirring sight as they sped past us on their way to attack enemy shipping off the coast of Holland. With their bows lifted high and huge plumes of white spray streaming behind their dark hulls they would cut through the silver path of moonlight, sending sparkling waves dancing in their wake. At dawn, they would come slowly back through the narrow entrance into the dock, with the signs of conflict on their splintered hulls and often with the ensign at half mast.

With the air offensive by both night and day increasing steadily, we too were going to be busy, and much sooner than we realised.

Flotilla in line ahead en route to Dartmouth

CHAPTER 14

Straight to Business

'Coxswain, all hands turn to. Out fires and harbour stations!'

The coxswain, emerging from his cabin below the midships hatch, looked up at me in amazement as I stood at the head of the companion. We had only just arrived in Felixstowe and the crew, who had only a few minutes before secured our ropes and been allowed below, were relaxing over a cup of 'char'.

'Are we fuelling sir?' he asked, since the coal fires in the wardroom, galley and crew's messdeck always had to be put completely out before going to fill up the tanks with petrol. (The danger of explosion meant that we had to be extremely careful about naked lights, and at all times no smoking was allowed aft of the bridge near the engine room and fuel tanks.)

'You heard me,' I replied. 'We're on immediate notice for sea.'

'Blimey! They haven't wasted much time, have they, sir?' he exclaimed, turning to enter the messdeck. 'Come on lads, out pipes, duty watch on deck.'

To a chorus of murmurings from the crew, facing the prospect of a cold supper, the embers of the fires were dowsed and the boat was warped out from her inside berth against the quay.

It had always been normal practice to refuel immediately on returning from patrol, but with all four boats having to queue for fuel and the need to report our arrival and get our bearings first, we had come straight into our new harbour. And we hadn't expected to enter the duty roster quite so quickly.

Some time later, having found our way to the RAF fuelling jetty just down river and replenished our water tanks as well, we were back alongside our companions and I was checking charts and preparing to carry out our orders to leave harbour early next morning on our first patrol from our new base.

At least there was no need for us to spend the night hours getting out to our patrol position in the narrower seas between Felixstowe and the Dutch coast. We could leave in the early morning and be out beyond the sandbanks which lie off the East Anglian coastline within a couple of hours. And most of the raids in that area were being made in daylight by American bombers protected by long range fighters.

There was no need any more for the long haul through the darkness down the Humber and out into the cold, lonely heart of the sea. Now it was a short run to the river mouth, in the rosy light of dawn, through the sand banks and past the Cork light vessel to a waiting position which was often within sight of land. The shallower waters showed a pale shade of green, often tinged with pale blues and pinks in the evening light. They could make things very unpleasant, however, when an easterly wind whipped them up into short, broken waves, giving the boat a rapid bumping, juddering motion, which made it very difficult to eat a meal, to plot a course or do any simple task.

We had a much busier base, as well. On the opposite side of the little harbour were the flotillas of MTBs and MGBs moored in large groups. Across the estuary, in Harwich, were flotillas of minesweepers, frigates and Hunt class destroyers, protecting the convoy route. There was a feeling of being back in the pukka navy, manning the fo'c'stle in white jerseys every time we entered and left the harbour.

Things had changed in other ways since we had last been in the North Sea. The American Eighth Air Force, 'The Mighty Eighth' as they came to be known, were making massive saturation attacks on the areas from which supplies might be sent to the Western front. With American efficiency and concern for the safety of their airmen, they had ensured that an effective pick-up system should be established, from which we were to benefit. We were able to lie near a buoy – on this morning it was the North Galloper, marking the Galloper Shoal – and wait for a vector instead of a distant and not always accurate position. That is to say, from a fixed position, we were given a bearing and distance to steer and the call sign of the search aircraft, making the whole process much simpler and more effective. In addition to the normal wireless watch, we always had a crew member operating the VHF set in the wheelhouse, passing messages up to the bridge and sending back our replies.

After reaching the Galloper at breakfast time, we had enjoyed a pleasant summer day, relaxing in the sunshine, and tea had just been handed around to the watch on deck, when a call came through.

'Vector 105 degrees, 18 miles.'

This was too easy. Off we sped at full speed. In calm water, we could expect to be there in about an hour. Within twenty minutes, however, Clem Woodhead, on VHF watch beside me in the wheelhouse, reported

'Teamwork 39 calling, sir. Dinghies bearing 045.'

Away to the North-East we could see an aircraft circling, so, adjusting our course, we headed towards what turned out to be a Thunderbolt fighter. The pilot dropped a smoke float to guide us and only ten minutes later we were alongside a pair of dinghies containing nine American airmen.

They were the survivors of Liberator L 2201 of 732 Bomb Squadron, 453 Bomb Group, captained by Lieutenant Prouhet. The tail gunner had unfortunately been killed, but the others were in good condition. They had taken part in a massive attack by 1048 bombers on Munich, with Augsburg as the subsidiary target. The strain being imposed on the Luftwaffe was obvious, because they were unopposed by German fighters, but over Munich they met an intense ack-ack barrage and received a hit which forced them to ditch before they could reach land.

Making them comfortable in the wardroom and sick bay, we debated whether this was indeed the ditching to which we had originally been called and we decided to make sure by heading towards the position we had been given earlier. This proved a wise move, as we soon received a message to contact a Supermarine Walrus aircraft, call sign Revive 24. From its pilot we learnt that a second Walrus had landed to pick up a survivor from a dinghy and was having difficulty in taking off again. The vector this time was 120 degrees 15 miles, which meant that before long we were able to contact the other Walrus by radio. By now, the sky had become overcast and a North-Westerly wind was whipping the sea into the short, choppy waves which are characteristic of this shallower part of the sea. Soon we spotted the aircraft, rising and falling and with wings swaying uncomfortably. Learning that the American survivor was severely injured, Andy told Doc Bowler to prepare a Neil Robertson stretcher. This is a stretcher used in mountain rescues, which consists of canvas reinforced by wooden slats running lengthways, so that it can be wrapped around the patient's body and strapped tightly, holding him rigid whilst he is lifted by ropes at each end.

'The fuselage is too short and too low for us to go in bows-on,' said Andy. 'The only way we can get him inboard is to tuck the stern in gently against the after cockpit.'

Lieut. E. Smith on bridge of RML 520

The Walrus was a small amphibian biplane, with a short, boat-shaped hull and a pair of wings mounted above the fuselage. It had retractable wheels to enable it to operate from land. Between the wings was a single pusher-type engine, with the propeller at the rear, and there were floats under each wing to keep it stable when it was stopped. There were open cockpits with machine guns right up in the bow and behind the wings, and a covered cockpit just in front of the wings for the pilot and the observer. In fact, it looked much more like a relic from the first world war than a modern aircraft. It was quite useful, however, for Air-Sea Rescue, provided the sea was calm, because then it could land and taxi right up to a dinghy. The survivor could then be hauled quite easily into one of the cockpits, since there was very little freeboard above the surface of the water. From June 1944, a special ASR Squadron of the Fleet Air Arm, number 278, started operating from Martlesham Heath in Essex.

Since the overall length was only 37 feet, there would be only just enough room to manoeuvre stern first alongside the rear of the port wing, and place our counter, the lowest part of the boat, against the fuselage. I took our strongest lads, Goodwin, Wilson, Boswell and Banks down aft, whilst the coxswain handled the wheel. Very delicately, Andy brought the stern in, enabling Bowler to take advantage of a favourable wave to slip over the stern guardrail and down into the rear cockpit. With the airmen's help, he strapped the injured man into the stretcher and the ropes were passed up to us on the deck above. Anyone who has experienced the difficulty of getting out of a boat which is being lifted and dropped on the heaving waves will appreciate the difficulty we had in hoisting him inboard. I remember sharing his agony when our stern surged up high above the plane for a moment, carrying him clear of the fuselage. He hung swaying in mid air, and crying out in pain, before plunging downwards again as we struggled to haul in the ropes. It took us all our strength to lift him at last on to the after deck. It was a relief to all of us when he was finally settled, as comfortably as was possible, in the sick bay, with his wounds attended to.

The Walrus crew decided to make another effort to take off, whilst we stood by in case of trouble. As it gathered speed into the wind, the Walrus began to bounce uncontrollably and it was obviously in danger of breaking up or plunging nose first into the waves. The pilot wisely throttled back and waited for us to come to him. He had decided to accept our hospitality, so once again we manoeuvred alongside, this time passing a line into the for'ard cockpit and fastening a tow-rope, by means of a shackle, to the towing bolt in the plane's nose. When all was secure, the two airmen climbed aboard and we began to tow.

By this time, HSL 2578 had arrived on the scene. They took over the search for the remainder of the aircrew, as bodies had been reported floating in the area. They did indeed find five bodies but unfortunately no more survivors. Meanwhile, with our two British and ten Americans, not forgetting the salvaged Walrus, we headed back to Felixstowe.

Inside the Galloper shoal, where the sea was calmer, we were met by another HSL, 2572, and handed over the Walrus to her so as to get our survivors ashore as soon as possible. It was not until the early hours of the morning, after refuelling ready for our next outing, that we were able to secure snugly in our berth and get some rest.

But that gave us nothing to complain about, considering the success of our first day in Felixstowe, with a triple rescue and a salvaged aircraft into the bargain. We went around to the RAF base next day to survey with pride our Walrus, which had been brought up the slipway to the apron in front of the hangars. We felt we had certainly given *Beehive* something to buzz about.

It was heartening, too, to be part of such an improved ASR set-up. The Thunderbolts were able to cover the whole area rapidly in co-ordinated sweeps, and were easily contacted. In addition, the new Warwick aircraft, specially designed for carrying lifeboats, accompanied every raid as flying ops rooms, shepherding damaged aircraft to safety. They kept in contact with both the returning bombers and the search aircraft as well as our boats, dropping a lifeboat where necessary and directing rescue launches to the spot. The long delays in communication with Nore HQ and the lack of information were becoming a thing of the past, as was also the casual use of untrained and badly-briefed aircrews. In the remainder of that month of July, 1944, our small flotilla rescued altogether 26 survivors from 7 aircraft, including the crew of yet another Walrus.

CHAPTER 15

The Great Walrus Hunt

There is a pub in Plymouth called the *Walrus*, with a sign depicting the walrus from *Alice in Wonderland*. Which is a pity, because originally, when the pub was built just after the war, the sign showed a Walrus aircraft, described in the last chapter.

Someone with no feeling for naval tradition has recently chosen to wipe out the memory of the little Fleet Air Arm amphibian which played such a useful role in our area of the North Sea in the last year of the war. We had a number of encounters with them, often having to rescue the crew as well as the survivors they had gone down to pick up. They were obviously very useful search aircraft, since they could fly low and at a moderate speed and cover so much more sea than our launches; and in an emergency they could get to a ditching in a fraction of the time we would take. But they must have been expensive in terms of damage and losses, to judge from the number of incidents in which our flotilla alone was involved.

On the last day of July it was 520's turn to join the Walrus hunt. They had already carried out two successful rescues of survivors from American bombers on the 20th and 21st. On this occasion, at nine in the evening, after a day on patrol, Eddie Smith was expecting to be recalled, since all was quiet. Instead, there came a vector directing him 15 miles North-east to assist a Walrus which had rescued a Fortress crew. How the nine Americans had been stowed in the tiny plane it is impossible to imagine. They must have been sitting in rows along the wings, or crammed like sardines along the length of the fuselage. Certainly, with so much extra weight and a choppy sea as well, there was no hope of taking off. The pilot had called up their base to request assistance and was trying to taxi back westwards on the surface.

Dermot Barton worked out an interception course and, within an hour, the Walrus came in sight. All nine Americans and the two Naval airmen were taken on board 520 and brought back, with the Walrus in tow, to Felixstowe. Well before midnight 520 was back in harbour, the airmen had been landed and the plane was in the RAF hangar. Nothing could have been easier, thanks to the new improved ASR system.

It wasn't quite so simple for Sheppard when 550 went Walrussing too. It all began in the usual way: an order to head East for 33 miles, to rescue a Mustang pilot who had been shot down whilst on a strike over the island of Walcheren. He was met by Thunderbolt fighters who continually swept over him, guiding him towards their colleague, although for some reason he was unable to get clear reception of their voices over the VHF intercom.

Eventually Shep spotted red Very flares and the flashing of an Aldis signalling lamp, which he could see was coming from a dark shape on the horizon. This turned out to be a Walrus, lying on its side, with a broken wing. He headed towards it at maximum speed, pitching heavily into a sea which was growing increasingly rough, so that the plane was obviously in danger of sinking. As he circled the Walrus, however, Shep saw a yellow object some distance away, which he realised was the fighter pilot, lying motionless and unconscious in the waves. He had, in fact, been hit by the wing of the aircraft as it manoeuvred alongside him, and now he was in danger of being swamped by the waves and drowned.

Faced by the problem of saving the helpless American and also the Walrus crew, who were having to shift position constantly as the plane lurched further over on to its side and its bow sank deeper, Shep took an instant decision.

'Take over command Number One,' he ordered. 'You see to the Walrus, I'll get the Yank.'

He was a large man and a strong swimmer so, stripping off his outer gear, he dived from the bridge over the port side rail to swim to the fighter pilot. Reaching him, and keeping his head above water, he slowly fought his way back towards the boat, shouting instructions as he did so to his first lieutenant, who was a temporary replacement from the base.

Spike Gill, the gunner, who had been standing by the port boom with a heaving line, seized the lifebelt from the side of the bridge and threw it to Shep, who got an arm through it, enabling him to be pulled to the netting and helped aboard with the airman. The calcium flare attached to the lifebelt had ignited and the flame had been close to the back of Shep's head, which Spike rather unfeelingly thought was funny at the time.

As Shep had dived into the sea, the Walrus, which had been rocking heavily, suddenly took a plunge, its tail went up in the air, the nose went under and in a few moments it had gone. Spike heard a shout from the starboard side:

'Help me! I can't swim!'

It was the observer, who had been obliged to jump into the sea, together with the pilot, and who was floundering in the water, unable to get to the ship. The coxswain and motor mechanic launched one of the inflatable dinghies which our boats carried in case of emergency, and hoisted him into the dinghy. Meanwhile Spike, transferring his attention to the pilot, got his heaving line to him and, with the help of his shipmate, 'Taffy' Beck, went down the netting to haul him aboard.

With everyone safely on board, dried off and restored to normality by a generous helping of pusser's rum, they headed for home. Shep was later to get the MBE for this exploit.

Only three days later, 520 re-enacted almost the same drama in the same spot, but late in the evening, so that it was complicated by the darkness of the night. It was not until eight o'clock that the signal came through vectoring them 060 degrees 30 miles from their waiting position 18 miles East of Orfordness. They were told that a P-38 Lightning pilot was reported to have sent out a Mayday 40 miles East of Aldeburgh and flares had been sighted in this area.

By the time they had reached the spot darkness had fallen, so Eddie had to search as well as was possible with the aid of the bridge searchlight and star shell from the rocket guns.

'Do you think there's any hope of seeing a dinghy in this light, sir?' asked his coxswain, as the whole crew peered into the surrounding darkness, lit fitfully by the white glow of falling flares.

'If he sees we're searching for him, and fires a Very cartridge, there's every chance of finding him,' replied Eddie. 'Keep looking, everyone.'

As the search continued, the weather began rapidly to get worse. A force six wind had sprung up from the East, raising a heavy swell and a rough sea. It was just beginning to seem that trying to do a box search under these conditions was hopeless when the starboard lookout spotted, through his night glasses, lights to the northward.

'There's another boat searching off our beam, sir,' he said. 'I think I can see her navigation lights and she's using a searchlight.'

Eddie studied the flashes coming intermittently from the dark horizon.

'That's not a searchlight, it's a signal lamp,' he said. 'It could be MGBs or E-boats. We can't take any risks. Hands to action stations! Starboard twenty coxswain. Number one, send the challenge.'

Dermot checked the code for the day and flashed the letter with his Aldis lamp. Then, as they closed the mystery vessel, he read the reply:

'SOS. Be quick!'

Still maintaining their precautions, they increased speed towards the lights.

'Blimey!' exclaimed the coxswain, as they drew nearer. 'It's not a boat, it's a bloody Walrus!'

'Hurry, please!' cried a voice across the water. 'We can't last much longer, she's breaking up fast.'

Sizing up the situation, Eddie realised that the wind and the swell were far too strong for him to risk coming alongside. He could easily crush the fragile little plane beneath his plunging bow. So he manoeuvred the boat to windward of the Walrus, to protect it from the worst of the weather, and ordered two of the inflatable dinghies which were carried in the bow locker, to be got ready, with lines attached.

'I'm floating two dinghies down to you,' he called, using the loud hailer attached to the mast. 'Jump in, and we'll haul you to us.'

Unfortunately, the boat was rolling so heavily that the whiplash on the lines caused them to snap and the dinghies were swept away before the airmen could get into them. However, as the boat was carried by the wind towards the plane, the crew were able to throw a number of heaving lines across the fuselage. Grasping these, the two airmen waited for a favourable wave to lift them close to the ship's deck and jumped. As the ship rolled to meet the rising wing, the pilot managed to time his leap just well enough to grasp the guardrail and be seized by two of 520's crew. He was rapidly hauled inboard, but the observer, mistiming his jump, fell into the water. Luckily, he clung on tight to his lifeline and, as the swell lifted him again, he was hauled to safety. Then the lines which had straddled the Walrus were cut and she was swept away by the wind.

Apparently it was the Walrus crew which had reported seeing lights on the water. They had landed and searched for an hour, until darkness began to fall. Then, with the worsening weather, they had been unable to take off and been obliged to wait and hope that they would survive the storm and be contacted at daylight.

The Lightning pilot still had to be found, of course, so Eddie continued his search throughout the night. At daylight he was joined by two Thunderbolts and a Warwick, but their combined efforts still failed to produce any sign of the missing airman. The two inflatable dinghies which had broken adrift from 520 were recovered 11 miles to the South-West of the original position. And the Walrus was discovered, incredibly still afloat and with less damage than it had appeared, in the darkness, to have suffered, no less than 16 miles to the South-West! It emphasised again the powerful effect of wind and sea on a floating object and showed how far a dinghy could be driven from its original position in the interval between ditching and a search being organised.

Once again, Eddie had bagged a prize, to put him one up on the rest of us. But not for long. As 520 was returning to Felixstowe, on the 13th of September, 550 had already set out to take her turn in the constant patrol which had to be kept up as the fighters and bombers maintained the offensive against the retreating enemy. The allies were now striking into Belgium and Holland, only just across the water.

Once again a Lightning pilot was reported as sending out a mayday call East of Aldeburgh, and again a Walrus landed, picking him up this time. The reports do not make clear whether this was the same pilot as had ditched the previous day, but it may well have been another, since there was so much activity over the low countries. However, Sheppard was directed to come to the aid of the Walrus, since the previous night's storm had not fully died down. Eight to ten-foot waves made it impossible for the seaplane to take off so, once again, the crew and their American survivor took passage with Shep and another Walrus was delivered intact to Felixstowe for return to Martlesham.

Looking back on these rescues it seems odd that in each case the boat was forced to do a tricky manoeuvre in order to take the crew off the seaplane. Those who fell into the sea might easily have been swept away and drowned and the others could have been lost if the plane had sunk before we could reach them. It seems incredible that those chaps could have taken such risks without carrying a dinghy themselves. They seem to have had a very misplaced confidence in the seaworthiness of their plane.

This was borne out by our next encounter, about three weeks later, when only Andy's skilful handling of the ship prevented the loss of at least one life. We were on our way out to our patrol position when we were vectored on to a ditching. We had been having engine trouble, but our motor mechanic, PO Mason, quickly got us going again, and we were soon heading at full revs along the bearing we had been given.

'Have you heard the buzz?' said Boswell to his assistant gunner, Evans, a pale and rather undernourished cockney, who came in for a bit of mickey-taking from his mates.

'Naow, what?' was the anxious reply.

'There's a Walrus ahead!'

'Garn,' growled Evans, 'What you on about? Jimmy just told us. There's been three of them fighters already all saying the same thing.'

In fact, we now seemed to be over-supplied with support aircraft. We had had three separate messages that just ahead of us a Walrus was going down to pick up a fighter pilot from a one-man dinghy. A naval trawler was said to be standing by, but obviously experience had shown that there could be problems which only we would be able to deal with. So we carried on, very soon spotting the trawler – the *George Adgell* – with the Walrus close by.

'Walrus reports the airman is now in the trawler,' called Clem Woodhead, on VHF watch in the wheelhouse. 'Stand clear, about to take off.'

'You hope,' murmured someone behind me, as the little plane taxied into the wind and began its run. We remained at a distance, watching anxiously.

An easterly wind had gradually increased in strength since the rescue had taken place and it was blowing the spray off the white horses which fringed the short, choppy waves into which the Walrus had to fly, working up to maximum speed in order to take off. As it scudded across the wave-crests, it started to bounce more and more heavily, sending up sheets of spray around its wings, as it dug ever deeper into the surface at every bounce. The buffeting was more than its frame could endure. Suddenly one wing dipped, the other rose in the air, and it keeled over and slewed round to port.

'It dipped its port wing,' I exclaimed. ' It looks as if the float's ripped off.'

This was indeed what had happened. Fortunately, however, before the plane could capsize, the pilot had throttled back his engine and brought it to a stop, listing badly, with its lower port wing under the water looking like a wounded bird.

'Full ahead,' said Andy. 'We'll close her. They'll not be able to take off now.'

'Wilson, Ainsworth, stand by with heaving lines. Boswell, Evans, get fenders,' I ordered. 'Goodwin, bring a dinghy up to the bow.'

'We'll come alongside her bow,' said Andy, seeing the pilot climb out of the for'ard cockpit as we approached from the port side of the aircraft. 'Slow ahead, starboard ten . . . midships . . . steady as she goes. Stop both. Slow astern port. Stop engines.'

Carefully, he placed our bow just ahead of the plane's bow and brought it under our lee.

There was no need of heaving lines or even fenders. The pilot, taking advantage of a rising wave, was able to grab the guardrail and get a foot on to the ship's sidestrake, amidships. We were then able to help him over the rail without too much difficulty.

The Walrus was floundering badly, however, and taking on a steeper list, which threatened the life of the observer, who had clambered out on to the starboard wing as the fuselage filled with seawater and started to sink by the stern. His situation looked extremely precarious. He was half-kneeling on the upper wing, clinging to the edge to avoid slipping down the increasing incline. Using the engines to swing the stern clear and then come swiftly around to starboard, Andy thrust the bow of 547 neatly up against the wing-tip, which was just high enough to form a kind of gang-plank on to the point of our bow. It was so impressive that I can still picture the airman rising to his feet and simply stepping aboard: there was only a very low rail on the fo'c'stle so as not to obstruct the field of fire from the pom-pom.

It was only just in time, however, for, as we pulled astern to clear the wreck, the wing rose high in the air and the aircraft gave a sudden lurch and began to sink. Within a few minutes it had disappeared beneath the waves.

After staying out on patrol for some hours, we were recalled, returning to harbour rather miffed at not having another towed-in Walrus to add to the tally. But at least honours were even between the three of us.

Doug Tratner and 553 missed out on the Walrus hunt because they were undergoing a refit about this time. They did, however, come in one day with a tall story which they milked to the full, 'swinging the lamp' at wardroom parties for some time afterwards. They claimed to have been lying just off Orfordness one sunny afternoon, in a dead flat calm, when Doug, gazing idly around the horizon, suddenly saw a periscope slowly rise up before his astonished eyes, only a few cables' lengths away.

'There it was,' Doug would say, eyes wide and staring to illustrate his surprise, 'sticking out of the water, not moving an inch. Then it turned slowly around, and sighted us. It stopped for a second or two, looking at us, and promptly disappeared. I ordered depth charges ready, and put in an attack, but it must have slipped away.'

None of us drank at sea, and Doug was a very steady sort of fellow. It has been revealed, since the war, that German mini-submarines were tried out in the North Sea, so maybe this was one of them. On the other hand it was always useful to find an excuse to drop a depth charge. The fresh fish which rose to the surface afterwards were absolutely delicious! And the yarn did help to divert attention from our own and Shep's line-shooting about our salvage exploits. It has occurred to me since that we might have put in a salvage claim on those aircraft and earned a fortune. But it must be too late now!

CHAPTER 16

Market Garden

It had to be one of the worst-kept secrets of the war. Early in September every boat was issued with a fat envelope containing sealed orders, which lay around for day after day. It was a great temptation to open it and find out what was brewing as, almost every day, we were ordered to stand by, for something mysteriously code-named 'Market Garden', and almost every evening the operation, whatever it was, was postponed. At airfields all over the South of England thousands of men were getting impatient as they were told first it was on, then it was off, then on again. No doubt many of those sealed envelopes were opened and people must have been talking about it for days before it happened.

The name itself pointed to something happening on the flat plains of Holland, where air activity had been greatly stepped up, as our own large number of rescues in September showed. What we were all waiting for was, of course, the now famous Arnhem adventure. The top brass tried later to excuse the failure of the expedition by claiming that a Panzer division was unexpectedly resting in the area. That takes a lot of believing, when you consider the damage to security caused by the constant postponements and the amount of information our aircraft must have brought back. The Germans must have been expecting something to happen and been to some extent prepared.

At last, on the 15th of September, we got the green light and in the early hours of the 16th, in obedience to our special instructions, we all sailed out in line ahead, due East for the coast of Holland. On the way, we dropped our companions one by one at their patrol points, until 547 was left on its own to take up position, about noon, a few miles from the island of Walcheren, and roughly 70 miles from Felixstowe. A red buoy, marking the approach to the Scheldt, and the spire of Domburg church, standing out above the long low coastline, gave us an easy check on our position. Everything was still and a flat, calm sea enabled us to stop engines and lie to in comfort. Guns were manned, of course, and eyes kept peeled for any sign of the enemy, but nothing was happening to disturb the peace of a perfect autumn day.

It was a strange feeling, to be lying unchallenged, in broad daylight, within a gun-shot of the enemy, in waters which had so recently been the scene of violent night actions between our boats from *Beehive* and well-protected enemy convoys.

'Where are we?' asked Greenwood, in surprise, as he came on deck with a plate of roast beef and two veg for Andy's lunch.

'See that church spire?' said Tom Goodwin, who was standing by the starboard Lewis gun. 'There's a Jerry up there, got you in his sights. Don't hang about, I want my dinner before he starts shooting.'

The chef's jaw dropped, and he scuttled back down to his galley. All remained quiet, however, and he was able to carry on serving up the substantial eats provided by Flash Speed's efficient catering service.

To the North of us, RML 498, from the Yarmouth flotilla, could be seen, and 520 lay just visible on the Western horizon. We were the last of a long, double line of both RAF and naval ASR launches stretching right back to Orfordness. Each boat was visible to its neighbours, so that, throughout a wide stretch of sea, nothing could fall from the sky without being spotted by at least two boats.

Having completed my log and made certain of the accuracy of our position, I had just sat down on the step aft of the bridge, with my plate of food on my knees, when the sudden cry of 'Aircraft bearing Red nine-o' made me jump up and almost send my dinner flying over the side.

Looking westward into the heat haze which covered the sky, we watched in amazement as squadron after squadron emerged from the mist to fill the entire sky with a vast aerial armada. Huge formations of silver Liberators, thousands of feet deep and broad glistened in the sunlight. These were followed by masses of Dakotas, glider tugs and gliders, with fighter escorts circling above and around them. Slowly and majestically, with no sign of interference from the enemy, an endless stream sailed low overhead, darkening the sun as they followed the pathway we had marked out across the sea. We had seen large numbers of Fortresses flying in tight formations on raids into Germany, and RAF thousand bomber streams forming up above us, but this was on an altogether different scale. Tightly packed, at carefully regulated levels of height, they lumbered steadily over the pale green carpet of the sea into the heart of enemy held Holland. We know now how hot a reception they were going to get by the time they reached their objective, but nothing seemed to stir on the shore, no firing, no fighter opposition and no enemy boats to attack those of us who had come so near to the coastline.

In *A Bridge Too Far*, Cornelius Ryan describes how, at the controls of a plane towing one of the Horsa gliders, Flight Sergeant William Thompson was looking down on the long line of launches set out like stepping stones to guide him across the sea. For a brief thirty minutes he could relax, with his navigation done for him. Lieutenant Hay, in a plane attached to a fact-gathering liaison unit, saw two downed gliders and another ditching. Tapping his corporal on the shoulder, he shouted, 'Have a look down there, Hobkirk.' Seeing the latter's anxious face as he glanced down, he rapidly added, 'There's nothing to worry about. Look at the boats already picking them up.'

Another glider pilot, Staff Sergeant Kitchener, watched in admiration the speed with which an Air-Sea Rescue launch came alongside a floating glider.

'They picked the men up so fast I don't think they even got their feet wet,' he said later.

It was the busiest afternoon the ASR service ever had, throughout the war. Hardly any boat failed to pick up a glider's crew or two. Quite possibly it was 547 that Sergeant Kitchener saw, for suddenly, just before one o'clock, about six miles South-West of us, a glider broke its tow and started to drop away from its tug, circling lower and lower. There was nothing its pilot could do to avoid ditching.

Taff Williams had just poked his head out of the engine-room hatch, to get a view of the amazing scene, and was gazing open-mouthed into the sky.

'Get below,' I shouted, as Andy ordered full speed ahead towards it and I sprang to the compass to get its bearing and log the course.

Before we could hope to reach it, the glider had ditched and was already being circled by a crowd of aircraft: Spitfires, a Wellington and a Warwick, which dropped smoke floats to mark its position. Seeing us coming, the Warwick then kept up a patrol between us and the glider, whilst we anxiously watched the dark shape which we could now see floating on the surface. Would the men get out in time? Would it sink before we could get there? These were the anxious thoughts which kept us on tenterhooks as, all too slowly it seemed, in spite of cramming on extra revs, we hurried to the rescue. After a long, twenty minutes, with less than a mile to go, we saw it start to disappear.

'Blast it, she's going,' groaned Andy, watching through his binoculars. 'There's a dinghy though. Stand by the boom.'

We could now see that a number of men had got clear and were sitting in a dinghy. Within a few minutes they were being helped up the scrambling nets and brought aboard. They had indeed scarcely got their feet wet!

The whole crew of the glider had got safely away, but a jeep and two motor bikes had been lost to the invasion force. There were two members of the Glider Pilot Regiment and three of the First Para Regiment, one of whom, CQMS Cook already held the DSM. They were furious about missing the show and wanted to be put ashore on Walcheren, so that they could try to make it on their own to the dropping zone. This wasn't really on, of course, and it made more sense for them to go over with the next wave, which they probably did. We were, however, quite close to the shore by now, and could get a fix on Westkapelle church tower, as well as that of Domburg.

There was still no end to the procession of aircraft and gliders as we waited for some more guests to drop in on us. We could see other boats busy with ditchings away to the westward, but for the time none came our way. Then, about 1540, our companion on the end of the line, RML 498, was called up by the Warwick directing the rescue operations and she disappeared to the North-east.

A pair of 'Teamwork' Thunderbolts were pinpointing ditchings and reporting back to the co-ordinator in the Warwick. By listening to their chatter we learnt that 498 had gone to pick up a crew which had ditched rather inconveniently close inshore around the northern tip of Walcheren island. She was now coming under fire from shore batteries 10 miles North of Domburg, and the fighter pilots were going in to attack the enemy guns. We got her position, course and speed from the pilots and I rapidly worked out an interception course to go to her aid. About twenty minutes later we joined her, to find she had succeeded in picking up eight survivors. Meanwhile the fighter attacks had silenced the gunfire and the danger had passed. So, even if we had wanted to, which was far from our thoughts at the time, we weren't able to add an RML crew to our tally of rescues. We did, a few days later, obtain some rather good aerial photographs of the glider rescue as a souvenir, together with a complimentary letter from the Officer Commanding RAF Station, Langham, where the Warwicks were based.

Jerry's reaction to this invasion of his airspace was to step up the V1 and V2 barrage, which he had been sending across our stretch of the North Sea ever since the launch sites in France had been overrun. When we were anywhere near the Dutch coast, we not only used to see the buzz-bombs going over towards the West, but, on a clear day, the trails left by the V2 rockets as they went up from their launch pads far away to the East. When the last of the gliders had gone over and the towing and supply aircraft had returned, and the sky was clear again, we were recalled. Behind us in the fading light we could see the rocket trails going up and later, as darkness fell, the buzz-bombs overtook us, with their flaring jet engines. All along the East coast, as we approached, there was a grand firework display as the ack-ack batteries hammered away at the flying bombs, accompanied by huge explosions as they were knocked out of the sky.

We ourselves were not allowed to shoot at them, since our guns were not powerful enough to explode them, but might influence their course and speed, which was so predictable that they eventually became easy targets for the ack-ack gunners. I must confess, though, that we could not resist taking a pot-shot at one which came temptingly low and close. Boswell leapt eagerly into the turret and let off a few rounds, but it was already speeding past and away.

Having been the furthest out, we were the last back. By the time we had landed our paratroopers and refuelled ready for next day, it was not until the early hours of the morning that we were able to secure in harbour.

It was possible, however, to get a little sleep, since we were not required to go as far next morning. We were kept inshore, near Sunk Head Fort, a defence tower protecting the entrance

Glider, with crew in dinghy, September, 1944

to the Thames estuary, resembling very much the oil platforms which have since been built all over the North Sea. What a different situation would have been created in that empty expanse if all that oil had been discovered forty years earlier and needed to be protected!

In mid morning, however, the order came to proceed again to our station off Walcheren. We thought that perhaps we had been held back to ensure that we didn't arrive at our rather exposed position before there was air cover, or to avoid giving the enemy warning of another wave of airborne troops. The reason for the delay was, however, fog over the airfields, the problem which was going to become crucial in the next few days. Now, as we headed eastwards, more Liberators and Dakotas, some with supplies, some towing gliders, began to pass overhead, with Spitfires, Thunderbolts and Lightnings to protect them. We were encountering an increasing headwind of force four or five, with a sea to match, which meant that things were not too comfortable for us and a lot less easy for the glider pilots than on the previous day. However, the delay had produced one advantage: the Luftwaffe, which had been sent up on patrol all the morning, had returned to their base when the day's lift went in.

Soon the inevitable happened. A glider broke loose and went down away to the North-East of us. Once again it was maximum speed and a bouncy ride in the wheelhouse for me as we headed towards what we thought would be another quick pick-up. However, much of the line of boats was already established and an aircraft which had already begun to orbit the ditched glider had called two HSLs to the spot.

Only fifteen minutes later, as we continued on our original course, another glider fell out of the sky, to ditch right beside another HSL. Ten minutes after this, we sighted yet another ditching, attended by two more boats. We wondered whether there would be any left for us by the time Walcheren was reached.

'This is just the sort of thing I was suggesting when I visited that American airfield,' said Andy, as we went further on our way. 'A line of patrol boats that an aircraft in trouble could contact by VHF. They could pass him from boat to boat and, if he had to ditch, he could pick the nearest one. It might even help to get him back to land.' With a laugh he added, 'Do you remember that damaged bomber we contacted? How we talked him across, and when he reached the coast he said "Thanks for the buggy ride"? That saved both a plane and a crew.

547 picking up glider crew

'They're certainly going to need to ditch close to a boat today,' I replied, 'The wind's getting up, and it won't be easy to get to a glider in time.'

In our efforts to reach our destination as soon as possible, we were pitching heavily into the oncoming waves, which were getting higher as the wind increased. The pounding it was receiving eventually caused the pom-pom to break loose. As the bow pitched and rolled, it started to swing wildly from side to side, and we had to reduce speed whilst Boswell, Wilson and I struggled to lash it securely to the mounting. We all got well and truly drenched by the waves breaking over the bow before the gun was secured and speed could be increased again. It was a quarter to five when we arrived back on station off Domburg.

But there was to be no time relax and dry ourselves off. Only ten minutes later we spotted an aircraft going down about four miles to the South-West. Other aircraft, which appeared to be Dakotas, began to circle above it as once again we sped to the rescue. Luckily, the plane stayed afloat long enough for the crew to get out the dinghy and we were soon able to pick them up. The heavy seas made it rather more difficult this time, and Wilson got another drenching as he went down with Goodwin into the dinghy to help them climb the netting and be hoisted on board.

The four men proved to be the crew of Dakota No. 43–15139 of 306 TCS Squadron of 442 Carrier Group of the US Army. Their experience typified the determination and heroism of the men we had seen passing overhead on that and the previous day, and gave a vivid example of what they had to go through.

They took off at 1240, towing a glider piloted by F/O Herbert Bollum, for a landing zone North of Eindhoven. Four hours later, at Breda, still 28 miles short of their target, they ran into an intense concentration of flak and the left engine was hit. But Lieutenant McCormick, the pilot, pressed on to the landing zone.

'There's smoke pouring from your left engine,' warned Bollum, as his glider was about to break away. The Dakota crew were unable to see this, but they could tell something was wrong, because the engine was running rough, and they were unable to feather it. As they crossed the Dutch coast, the plane was filling up with smoke.

'There are flames under the floor,' called Sgt Powell, the radio operator.

'Can you call up the others?' asked McCormick.

''Fraid not,' was the reply, 'the radio's out of action.'

'Get everyone to the rear of the plane,' ordered McCormick to his co-pilot, F/O Atterbury. 'If the fire gets worse, we'll have to ditch.'

Smoke was now pouring into the fuselage, so the pilot cut the mixture to the right engine in order to lose altitude.

'Stand by for ditching,' he called, nosing the plane down into a dive. As he did so he saw the hydraulic pressure gauge was indicating zero. The fire had burned away the hydraulic system and the landing gear was hanging down. As the plane lost height, he managed to pull it around into the wind and break the dive, slowing the speed enough to come in tail down, at about 80 mph. There was a shock as the tail hit the water, followed by a more violent impact when the nose hit. The sudden impact of landing tore the dinghy loose from its lashings and threw it forward in a tangled heap. There was no time to waste in untangling the dinghy and every possibility of an explosion.

'Jump clear!' McCormick shouted. 'Swim away from the plane!'

Dragging the dinghy with him, he followed the others out of the fuselage. They all had lifejackets, but could make no headway against the force of the sea, which was pinning them down between the trailing edge of the wing and the fuselage. They had to haul themselves along the edge of the wing until they reached the tip, which was bobbing up and down in the swell. Ducking underneath as it rose, they struggled clear of the leading edge, and floated away from the plane, managing to bring the dinghy with them. They were then able to inflate it and climb in, a remarkable feat in the circumstances. All that remained then was to wait a few minutes for us to arrive, by which time the aircraft had sunk.

McCormick had bruises and lacerations on his right leg and the radio operator had burns on his left hand and forearm, but the other two had no injuries. They were able to walk into their home mess the next evening to a joyful reception. Out of twenty aircraft which had set out on the 18th, eighteen had returned safely and one had crashed making an emergency landing, with injuries to only one of its crew. Our rescue provided a happy ending for one of that group's operations at least. In his report the Commanding Officer ended by saying:

'This was a rough month, but the Lord was riding with our gang.'

Whether the Lord was responsible for the weather which played havoc with the operations on the following days is another question. After the pick-up we were obliged to stay on patrol until the last of the aircraft had returned, steaming into the wind to ride out the storm, until an ASR Warwick passed on the message that we were to return to base. After an encounter with a floating mine, which we duly sank, we put McCormick and his crew ashore at midnight and prepared for another day on the Walcheren run.

We spent the next four days, however, on various waiting positions between Felixstowe and the Scheldt, covering the much more disjointed supply missions and fighter strikes. For most of the time thick fog hampered everyone's activities. On Tuesday the nineteenth, for example, the remaining eighteen planes of McCormick's group took off for the Eindhoven landing zone again, but ran into a wall of fog so thick that the gliders could not see their own tugs. The formation broke and dribbled back to base piecemeal, losing four gliders over the sea. Luckily, the crews were picked up, but not by us. We were enveloped in fog, too, and spent most of our time crawling around amidst the sandbanks of the Essex coast, gingerly feeling our way along the narrow and shallow channels with a leadsman in the bows, calling the soundings in the old-fashioned way:

'By the mark five' . . . 'And a half three' . . . Anything less could have spelt disaster.

We were at sea each day throughout the week, coping, like the airmen, with poor visibility and consequent frustration. But on the Saturday we thought we were on to something at last.

In the afternoon, as we were picking our way through the channels off the Blackwater estuary, a group of Dakotas broke out of the clouds ahead of us. Almost at once a chorus of voices greeted the appearance of a black object which fell from one of them and floated down on a red parachute. Flinging caution to the winds, Andy ordered full speed towards it, whilst I anxiously studied the chart for sandbanks and wrecks. A quick call brought support aircraft to the spot. Alas, it was a false alarm: it was only a supply parachute which had been accidentally released. So we returned to the monotony of patrol.

In the late evening, when the recall signal came, we were well to the South of Felixstowe and had to return via the swept channel of the inshore convoy route. With nightfall the visibility had improved, and we could see, some distance ahead, the navigation lights of low-flying bombers streaming eastwards. Occasionally a dark shape flew close to us and we recognised it as a Lancaster, heading no doubt for some bombing mission connected with the Arnhem battle. Andy and I were still both on watch, as careful navigation was still needed, and I was on the bridge looking out for the next buoy. Suddenly, as I gazed into the darkness, one of the lights exploded into a searing ball of flame and blazing debris arched into the sky, to fall and continue to burn on the surface of the water. The flames flickered for a while, then disappeared. Putting on speed, we loaded the rocket guns with star shell and illuminated the sea ahead of us. Within minutes we found ourselves in the midst of a large patch of oil and wreckage.

From official reports of that night's missing aircraft, it appears that it was a Lancaster, number NF 982B, of 101 Squadron, heading on a mission to Neuss. The cause is put down to a mid-air collision, although there is no report of a second aircraft being involved and it appeared to us that its bomb-load had simply exploded for some reason.

550, which had been following our stern light, now joined us and we swept the surface with our bridge projectors for signs of the crew. Presently the searchlight picked out what looked like two dark bundles of cloth floating in the oily water. The sound of waves breaking on a sandbank close to starboard sent me to check on our position, whilst the coxswain took charge of the gruesome duty of recovering, with the aid of heaving lines and boathooks, the mutilated remains of the two bodies. They were laid on the fo'c'stle in the cold glare of the searchlight, the raw white exposed bone of a torn-off limb imprinting on my mind an unforgettable image, which disturbed me, somehow, more than anything I had seen in the war before, in the blitzes and on Malta convoy in my days as an Ordinary Seaman. It seemed to stand as a vivid symbol of the horror of war, the way it dehumanised its victims, its indiscriminate slaughter.

We found in the clothing the means of identifying the bodies. One of them had a New Testament in his pocket, with an inscription which reflected his religious faith. The broken, barely human flesh seemed to mock his trust in a being who could allow this to happen to him, as a result not of enemy action even, but a chance accident. It brought back the memory of those survivors who had been so sure that there was something miraculous about their rescue. How could anyone, I felt, expect to be privileged to survive while others around him died? There was nothing original in this, of course. I suppose most of us found the only answer to fear was to resign ourselves to some form of fatalism and hope that we would come through.

We received orders from the base to bury the dead airmen at sea, but before we could complete our preparations for this unaccustomed task, we were told to bring them back for burial on shore. We were not very popular with the base staff when they came to remove the poor airmen's remains. Some time later I had a conversation with the Methodist minister in Felixstowe, who had had the difficult problem of reconciling the widow of the owner of the Testament to the tragedy of his death. And not only that: he had to persuade her not to insist on seeing his body.

We had seen at the beginning of the week one of the great spectacular events of the war, the Arnhem airlift, and, at the end, one small individual piece of the vast amount of suffering that was to be the result.

CHAPTER 17

Enter the Mighty Fourth

'The Mighty Fourth': that would have made a good title and a good subject for a film. The exploits of the American Fourth Fighter Group were outstanding. They put the punch into the air support for the Allied advance into Germany towards the end of 1944, and Douglas Fairbanks, either Senior or Junior, would have been the perfect actor to represent them. In fact, the pilot we were destined to meet up with that October was a Fairbanks double, and as tough as they come in anything Hollywood has produced.

Equipped with the vastly superior Mustang fighter, and carrying extra fuel tanks, which could be dropped when empty, they ranged wide over the battlefield and escorted the bombers deep into enemy territory. They covered daylight raids on Berlin, on aircraft factories and synthetic oil plants vital to German's survival. They forced Goering to withdraw squadrons from the Russian front and use the new jet fighter, the Me 163, in a desperate attempt to destroy the American fighter umbrella. In the war of attrition which followed, the Mighty Fourth proved a formidable opponent, wearing down the German defences by gradually removing their best pilots. They claimed over a thousand aircraft destroyed, the highest number of victories by any group, but they paid a heavy price themselves. Not only did they take on any odds, they often put themselves at risk by running the engine too long on boost in the heat of combat, so that they suffered engine failure and had to bale out. Or they stayed too long in a dogfight, leaving insufficient fuel to reach land. Searches now began to involve fighter pilots rather than bomber crews, as our last Walrus rescue had shown. And, unfortunately, it soon became evident that it was much harder for a fighter pilot to survive baling out into the sea, or for the rescue services to spot his tiny dinghy.

On October 7th, a squadron of nineteen Mustangs left Debden, in Suffolk, to escort a force of B-24s on a raid on Magdeburg. Over the Dutch coast, as they climbed to 20,000 feet, F/O Kenneth Foster, flying number three in Red section, noticed that his engine was overheating. The coolant temperature was rising fast and he could do nothing to stop it.

'Cobweb Red three to Red section leader,' he called. 'Engine overheating, returning to base, over.'

Behind him, Lt Renschler heard the call and saw him turn, with white smoke streaming out of both sides of his kite.

'Red four here,' he called, 'going down to cover Red three.'

Peeling off to follow him, he was just beginning to catch up when he saw the Mustang roll over and Foster bale out. At the same moment there was a huge fireball as the plane exploded and Foster disappeared in the smoke and flames. He saw the patch where the wreckage had hit the water, but there appeared to be no sign of his comrade. Two Thunderbolts responded to his mayday call, but though they searched for two hours they failed to spot a dinghy.

Foster, however, on seeing the smoke, had switched to the ASR channel and received an instant reply from 'Colgate', the tracking station:

Fighter pilot rescue, October 1944

'Calling Red three. Your position is Orfordness 65 miles, steer 270, keep contact, over.'

A moment later, the aircraft caught fire. Foster had to get out quickly.

'Red three to Colgate. I am on fire, baling out, over'.

'Roger Red three. Colgate here. Boat being sent, good luck, over and out,' was the final message.

Opening the canopy, and rolling the plane over, Foster found himself thrown partly out of the cockpit, with his legs stuck, due to the pressure of the slip stream against his body. With a desperate kick, he managed to free himself and the next instant found himself floating free in the air, flat on his back. It was his first jump, and rather a novel experience, he thought!

Twisting around, and seeing the sea rising to meet him, he realised that it was time to pull the ripcord and soon he was floating down smoothly, apparently unaware of his narrow escape from the explosion of his plane. As his feet hit the water, he hit the quick-release box of his parachute.

'Then,' he said later, 'began a silent struggle. I went under some distance and, having inflated my mae-west, I struggled to the top for air. As there was quite a swell running, and a few white caps, I was under water quite a bit. I found the carbon dioxide bottle, but because of the wool gloves I was wearing, had difficulty in locating the pin which allowed the valve to turn. Finally, after what seemed an eternity, I had the dinghy inflated and managed to crawl partially onto it. I rested there some moments and then began to make all seaworthy.'

So far luck and his own strength and determination had got him through the first difficulty of landing successfully. A frequent cause of drowning was becoming entangled in the straps of the parachute and being dragged under before it could be released. One of his comrades had recently suffered this fate. Now he had to endure the cold and discomfort of waiting to be seen and rescued, and there was no knowing how long this might take. Soon he was violently sick because of the seawater he had swallowed in the struggle to stay afloat. A little later he began to suffer seasickness, caused by the movement of the dinghy in the rough seas. Drenched by his ducking and chilled by the biting wind, he had violent fits of the shivers, which he overcame by working hard at baling out the dinghy and flailing his arms and beating his hands together.

His hopes rose, during the afternoon, when two Thunderbolts appeared. Taking out the two cartridge signals which he carried in his mae-west, he tried to fire them, but the soaking had made them useless, and the aircraft failed to see him.

As night fell, the sea began to grow calmer and he even managed, between fits of shivering, to get snatches of sleep. With the coming of day, he kept himself going by telling himself that help must come, but it was not until the afternoon that a sweep of four Thunderbolts appeared. This time they spotted him, circled and dropped smoke flares before flying back to the rescue launch, over the horizon, to guide it to him. However, he was to suffer a depth of disappointment such as I can only hope no unfortunate airman ever experienced on our account. The P-47s, possibly because of shortage of fuel, had to leave a Walrus to take over the search. It failed to spot him and, worse still, the rescue launch came within 400 yards without sighting him. He was elated at first, on seeing the launch so close that he could easily see the men standing on the deck, and he tried again to fire the three remaining cartridges from the dinghy case.

'They were all defective,' he said, 'and failed to fire, and I sat there and watched the boat move away to resume the search South of me.' We could imagine only too vividly how he must have felt.

Night came again, bringing rough seas and heavy rain. The dinghy covers failed to keep out the water and he had to bale frequently to keep down the amount of water in the bottom of the dinghy. But still he clung on to life and hope. He could hardly feel his cramped limbs, but he doggedly continued to exercise them as much as he was able, wriggling his toes and flexing his muscles to prevent them from stiffening up.

The morning of the third day dawned cloudy, with patches of fog lying around, but it soon brought renewed hope. He saw eight Thunderbolts go by on a sweep and one on the end passed close to him. Because of the rough water and poor visibility it failed to spot him but, twenty minutes later, they returned, flew over him and saw him. They began to circle but, because of the wind, they were carried away and lost him. Two boats appeared and stopped, again, like the day before, 400 yards away. Was it to be a repeat of yesterday's bitter disappointment?

On 547, we had spent the previous day, Sunday October 8th, being shunted about to various positions East of Felixstowe, without being called on to join in any searches. We had remained all the afternoon at Sunk Tower, with orders to await instructions, and had eventually been recalled to harbour. It might have helped if we had known exactly what had been going on when, at eleven o'clock that night, we were ordered to be at first light on a position 52.01.30 North and 02.47 East. HSL 2557 was to join us, which meant that, if we both sighted anything, the HSL, with her much greater speed, was likely to get to it first. But the tortoise sometimes manages to beat the hare.

Three o'clock in the morning saw us heading out of the estuary again, guided by the *Cork* light vessel, and eastwards to our rendez-vous, where we agreed with the HSL to do a 'key' search down wind. This meant searching long parallel strips of sea, first in a South-Easterly direction, then North-Westerly, then back to the South-East again, so as to cover a widening and at the same time lengthening area of sea. The sky was heavily overcast with a force four North-Easterly wind, and there was some rain about, but visibility at sea-level seemed reasonably good. At eight o'clock the eight Thunderbolts arrived and carried out a similar, but more extensive search, keeping in touch with us by VHF. Andy had the earphones on, listening to the chatter between the 'Teamwork' aircraft, whilst I kept the plot going on the wheelhouse chart table. We were on our fourth South-Easterly run when Andy called down to me, excitedly, 'They've sighted him. A dinghy with a man waving in it. Take this bearing. Aircraft circling South 10 East. It's about seven miles away. Coxswain, steer South 10 East. Engine room, full speed ahead.'

I rapidly marked the position on the plot, and registered our course and speed. Shortly afterwards, he called down, 'They've lost him again. They're all circling, but they can't see him. 2557's heading towards them. I'm altering course South by West. Mason,' he called down the engine-room voice-pipe, 'can't you get more speed on? They're going to beat us to it.'

As he watched the HSL moving swiftly towards the circling aircraft, and took bearings to keep a check on their position, Andy realised why they had lost the dinghy. The bearings were changing quite rapidly and in trying to follow them we were now heading South-South-West. He could see that, with no fixed point to relate to, and only sky and sea around them, the pilots were allowing themselves to be carried downwind without realising it. Each orbit they made was taking them further away from the dinghy which, being only about five feet by three feet and surrounded by waves, was drifting much less slowly. Experience had taught us how variously wind-drift could affect a floating object and Andy made use of this experience now. He ordered slow ahead to take stock of the situation, then he called, 'Alan, give me a course for the first position you plotted.'

'South 40 East,' I replied.

'Steer South 40 East, Coxswain, full ahead both,' he ordered. 'Keep a sharp lookout now, everyone.'

To all appearances we were heading off on a fool's errand, well away from all the other searchers. But Andy's judgement proved right. Only three minutes later, he sighted the dinghy dead ahead and just two hundred yards away. The tortoise had proved more cunning than the hare.

In another three minutes we were alongside the dinghy, with the boom out and the scrambling net down, and Goodwin and Wilson were ready to go down and lift the airman into the net.

'Boy, am I glad to see you!' he shouted, in true Hollywood style. 'Don't come down, I'm on my way up.'

We watched in amazement and admiration as he slowly, but doggedly forced his frozen limbs to climb the wide and swaying rope mesh virtually without any assistance and edged his way along the boom to the deck. Then he insisted on limping unaided to the sick bay. Only when he was inside did he allow Bowler to strip off his sea-soaked clothing and wash him clean of the unpleasant mess which had resulted from three days of sitting helplessly in the tiny dinghy. Normally, after forty-eight hours of immersion in seawater one would have expected the skin of his feet to have been in no state to allow him to climb or walk without damage to the flesh. Only will-power must have forced his stiffened muscles to act.

'I was given a good rub down and placed between wool blankets, with hot water bottles around me,' said Foster in his report. 'Soon after, when they saw I was in fairly good shape, I was given a hot cup of tea and a good shot of rum which, combined with the cheerfulness of my rescuers and my relief at being fished out, soon had me feeling quite myself again.'

What he did not reveal, except in a confidential chat with Andy, was that his chief concern, during the time he was sitting with his private parts soaking in a bath of icy seawater, was the effect it might have on his future performance. Would he ever again be able to rise to the occasion? For such a tough-looking, well-built man, with a film-star's pencil slim moustache and all the appearance of a typical Hollywood he-man, that would indeed have been a tragedy.

As he said, he was soon up again and enjoying his cruise, as we were ordered to remain at sea to cover further bomber and fighter sorties until the late evening, when we rather reluctantly put him ashore at *Beehive*.

On the 18th October, only two days after returning to his unit, Foster was back in action, supporting a force of B-17s on a mission to Cologne. He continued to fly with the Mighty Fourth until, on March 31st, 1945, he went down over Germany and became a prisoner of war. Fred Farington, who flew with him on that October day wrote to me to tell me that he died in about 1983, no doubt still with his functions unimpaired. He was a splendid example of the traditional tough guy and typical of the American airmen of world war two.

Foster's rescue was the last of a group of three rescues on virtually successive days. As we finally turned in to our bunks in the early hours of October 6th, after landing the Walrus crew, whose rescue was described earlier, Shep was preparing to put to sea on what proved to be a very special and not too comfortable mission. This time it was the unusual job of picking up an enemy aircrew before their own side could get to them.

With launch sites under attack, and more territory being occupied by the allies, the Germans had been obliged to find new ways of keeping up the buzz-bomb attacks on London. It was discovered that they had invented a means of launching them from Heinkel bombers, which flew a short distance into the North Sea and then sent them on their way over the Suffolk and Essex coasts towards London. Even as we were returning to Felixstowe with the Walrus crew, on October 5th, and only 36 hours before Foster baled out from his Mustang, one of these Heinkels was caught and shot down.

It was of course extremely important to get hold of any survivors, so that they could be interrogated to find out more about this new method of launching the V1 missiles. An intensive search at first light was soon successful, a Warwick aircraft reporting that it was circling a dinghy containing three of the German crew. Strangely enough, it was in almost exactly the same position as that in which Foster would bale out just a day later, about 40 miles due East of Felixstowe.

The duty boat replacing us was 550 so, at 0715 on the 6th, Sheppard was on his way. The weather, which had been gradually worsening the day before, had now started to reach gale force, which meant that it was too rough to send a faster HSL. In fact, Shep was given the option of returning if conditions were too rough. But he was told how important it was to get these men before their own ASR service could rescue them, so that they could be interrogated by our intelligence men. He was determined, therefore, to go ahead. On the way out of harbour, he gathered the crew around the bridge.

'There's a Heinkel down in the drink, and there are some survivors in a dinghy,' he told them. 'They were launching a flying bomb and the intelligence boys want us to bring back the survivors and as much of their gear as we can. It's the first known aircrew from one of these piggy-back jobs to survive, and we have to get them before their own lot does.'

Spike Gill was one of the crew members told to be armed and ready to search them and stand guard over them. He had already had one successful encounter with a Heinkel, when 550 had been in Lowestoft harbour, in 1942, before coming to Immingham. On that occasion, he had leapt to his Oerlikon as the air raid siren sounded and the loudspeaker on the quayside gave the warning 'Enemy raider approaching from the South-East.'

Almost immediately he saw the Heinkel swooping down out of the mist, approaching from the stern with machine-guns firing. Opening fire, he just had time to see that he had scored some hits before two bombs began to fall directly above him. Fortunately, they landed in the river without doing serious damage whilst the aircraft flew over the houses towards the sea with smoke and flames pouring from the fuselage.

Now Spike, armed with a service revolver, was keeping watch on the bridge as 550 corkscrewed and plunged into the heavy seas whipped up by the North-Easterly gale. As the morning went on, the weather grew steadily worse. The waves were crashing over the bow, hitting the wheelhouse and flooding over the open bridge. Speed had to be reduced and the boat began to suffer storm damage. Several fittings on the decks were smashed and six feet of the rubbing strake were carried away by the force of the waves hitting the port bow. To add to the danger, a drifting mine loomed up dead ahead. Fortunately it was spotted in time for Shep to take avoiding action. For some reason, Shep was unable to make contact with the Warwick which was orbiting the dinghy but, at about 1050, another Warwick flew past on its way to relieve the first one and they were able to get in touch on VHF. An hour later this pilot called Shep up to say that he was orbiting a man in the water. This put Shep in a dilemma: should he go first to the rescue of this man, who had no dinghy to support him? He reasoned, however, that as it would take over two hours to reach him, and his survival seemed extremely unlikely in those weather conditions, it was more practical to go on to the first and nearer target. Soon, a group of Spitfires got in touch with 550 and one of them came to check the course and distance to the dinghy, which was about ten miles away.

Ploughing on through the heavy seas, Shep at last sighted red Very's lights being fired from the surface dead ahead. He briefed his crew on the need to keep a constant watch on the Germans and not to speak to them. Shortly afterwards, Spike Gill, hoisting himself on to the flag locker, just caught sight of a Warwick circling ahead and glimpsed what appeared to be a yellow sail.

'Right, stand by rescue stations,' called Sheppard.

Spike, going to the port boom, wondered how, in those seas, they were going to be able to put out the scrambling nets without their being torn away. Then he saw the grey, boat-shaped German dinghy, with a small sail and two one-man dinghies trailing behind. In the larger dinghy were three men who attempted to ignore the lines thrown to them and refused to lower their sail. Shep manoeuvred as close to them as possible, turning beam-on to the sea in order to get them under his lee. The ship was rolling so heavily that the guardrails were going under the water. But this proved to be an advantage because, as the ship drifted down on to the dinghy and she rolled to port once again, the dinghy came rising up on the wave-crest close enough to be grabbed by Spike and his mates. As they rolled back to starboard, the German airmen came tumbling out on to the deck and were seized, searched and taken to the sick bay by Spike and the other guards. The dinghy itself had been grasped and made fast by a line to the guardrail.

When the rescued men had been stripped and bedded down in the sick bay, guarded by Spike and his mates, with loaded Smith and Wesson revolvers, Shep, who could speak a certain amount of German, came aft to tell them, 'You are on a ship of the Royal Navy, and prisoners of war. If you attempt to escape, the guard has orders to shoot you.'

They did not in fact display any further reluctance to co-operate. Indeed they were anxious to volunteer information about their two other comrades, one of whom appeared to be the airman spotted by the Warwick. They accepted meekly Shep's instructions not to speak to one another and remained quietly in their bunks, although they were quite fit and unhurt. Their names were: Klaus Schulte, Pilot, Heins Muller and Heins Weber, Air Gunners.

Shep then carried on to take up the search, with the Warwick, for their comrade. They spent four hours, in worsening weather conditions, searching the area without success. The sea was so rough, in fact, that the aircraft had difficulty in even seeing the RML, according to Shep, who had to fire flares to show where he was! At last they were recalled and ordered to take their prisoners to Parkeston Quay at Harwich and hand them over to the Intelligence Officer, before they could take their well-earned rest, around midnight, back in Felixstowe.

Although on this occasion the Germans would have been keen to prevent us from rescuing their airmen, there was a remarkable amount of mutual aid between us and the enemy, when lives were at stake and rescue by the crew's own side was impossible. There were occasions when the RAF put out a call on the international frequency, giving the position of a dinghy close to the Dutch or Danish coast, so that the German rescue service could find it. This made the occasional interference by trigger-happy pilots on either side all the more tragic. One HSL from Yarmouth was even badly shot up by a group of American fighters, whose pilots presumably assumed they were attacking an enemy boat. All but one of the crew were either killed or wounded.

A watch was also kept on the wave-lengths of the German fighter squadrons, so that their reports of shooting down aircraft over the sea could be noted and the rescue of the crews could be attempted. On one occasion, for example, a Messerschmitt pilot triumphantly gave the positions of two aircraft which he had just shot down and Coastal Command were able to send in airborne lifeboats in which the survivors were able to head westwards and meet surface vessels sent to intercept them.

It was obviously impossible for Shep to have remained another twenty-four hours on the position where he had picked up the Heinkel crew, but if he had done so he would have been very likely to have spotted Foster as he baled out, saving him a lot of discomfort. In fact there were a number of such swift rescues, made remarkably easy thanks to the improved efficiency of radio communication with search aircraft. It was sometimes a case of 'Don't come to me, I'll come to you!' Eddie Smith, for example, was lying one day at his waiting position when a B-24 appeared overhead, escorted by a Thunderbolt of the ASR service. The fighter pilot called him up on the VHF and asked him to follow the bomber until it ditched. He duly followed, at full speed, together with 512, which was in company with 520. Shortly afterwards they saw the plane hit the water about five miles ahead. A minesweeper, *HMS Cockatrice* also happened to be nearby and she launched a whaler to pick up four survivors, whilst Eddie found two and the other boat three. The whole crew was accounted for in very quick time, which was extremely fortunate, since the men had to cling on to pieces of wreckage to keep themselves afloat. Another ditching the next day was far less satisfactory. Eddie was led by a pair of Thunderbolts to an airman supported by a lifejacket which had been dropped to him by a Walrus that had been unable to land because of the weather. Of the other nine airmen, only one dead body was found.

Another example of the 'just drop in, we're waiting' type of fast customer service occurred during the Arnhem operation. Seeing a Dakota with a Thunderbolt escort flying low over the sea near his waiting position, Shep steered towards it and called up the escort.

'Hello Teamwork. Suggest you tell your Dakota, if he thinks he might not make it, to ditch while he still has control.'

The Dakota came nearer and Shep could see that the tail unit was badly damaged and the fuselage was badly holed, whilst the engine seemed to be misfiring. It circled lower over the boat and touched down on the surface only 100 yards away, making a perfect landing. It remained afloat for five minutes, enabling Shep to take off all the crew and pick up the dinghy, which they had been unable to use because it was upside down. A Walrus then passed the news of the rescue to a High Speed Launch, which came and took off the airmen, giving them a high speed delivery back to shore and to their base. It would have been hard to improve on that, even today.

There was a rather tall story told at wardroom parties, where the duty-free gin and whisky flowed freely, encouraging a certain amount of exaggeration, known in naval parlance as 'line-shooting' or 'swinging the lamp'. It concerned a pilot who had baled out over an RML and had been very annoyed at being made to hit the water alongside, instead of being allowed to land on the deck. It had to be pointed out to him that the many protuberances on the ship's deck could have given him a nasty jolt if he had come down on one of them.

Although, no doubt, the story was embroidered when it was recounted later for our benefit, RML 550 also made one of the most succinct and laconic official reports ever. It went as follows:

14.12.44 on way back to base after recall
1710 Red flare seen near North Galloper buoy
1730 Saw dinghy
1756 7 rescued
2050 Returned to base

Andy's earlier vision of a drop-in service was not far from being realised as the year reached its close.

CHAPTER 18

A Lucky Escape

'Christ! Jimmy's a gonner!' The startled cry from the fo'c'stle was followed immediately by a sickening crunch, which shocked every member of the crew.

That moment remains vividly fixed in my memory, where so much else has dissolved into hazy recollections of routine activities and general discomfort. I cannot even remember on which of those evenings it happened when, after returning late at night and landing our survivors, we dowsed our fires and went around to the RAF base to refuel. But I can still see ahead of me the shaded light over the white concrete jetty at the end of the long, narrow pier which jutted out into the estuary. I can see now its reflection on the black water lapping at the edge of the platform. An exceptionally high spring tide was at the flood, which meant that we were at the full height of the ship's side above the level of the concrete.

I was on the deck amidships, supervising the preparation of heaving lines and mooring ropes. From where I stood, I could see better than those on the bridge that the surface of the water was almost level with the edge of the jetty. What was more urgent was the realisation that we were being carried towards it too fast and too close, so that we were in danger of hitting the corner and being holed in the bow, right on the water-line.

'Fenders!' I shouted, picking up at the same time a small round 'pudding' fender and throwing it over the side. Holding the end of the rope and leaning out over the guard-rail, so as to swing the fender as low as possible in under the flare of the bow, I ran forward. My intention was to try to get the fender between the corner and the ship's side and to limit the damage. However, in the darkness and in my preoccupation with the task in hand, I did not realise that I had reached the point where the guard-rail was cut away to allow the traverse of the forward gun. I had nothing to support my weight. My impetus propelled me head first over the side and I disappeared from view just as the bow hit the concrete.

Hearing the crack as they met, everyone imagined that it was the crunching of bones that they could hear and a prayer or two went up for their mangled Number One. However, by chance, I had instinctively flung out my left hand and grabbed the wire of the lowered rail, momentarily checking my fall and turning my body over in a somersault which brought me upright again. I gave the left side of my face a bit of a crack against the wooden hull, but my legs had only a short distance to drop and I found myself sitting on a coil of old rope which had helped to break my fall. The overhang of the bow had also ensured that I had not fallen into the dreaded gap between the jetty and the ship's stem. Bemused, slightly shocked, but still intact, I looked up to see dim white faces peering down at me with startled fear and amazement in their eyes.

'We all thought it was you, sir, when we heard that crunching sound', said Boswell, who had jumped down to help me to my feet.

Speed also was at hand to connect up the fuelling hose and help me back on board, although how, in my dazed condition, I accomplished it is now erased from my memory. I have shuddered since to think of what might have been my fate, if I had fallen a moment sooner.

Fortunately there was no evident damage to the boat. But not long afterwards in our eagerness to add another rescue to our tally, we narrowly escaped disaster. Again a powerful tide was to blame.

A flood tide was running strongly, carrying us with it, as we headed southwards down one of the narrow channels which thread through the sandbanks off the Essex coast. E-boats, mines and air attacks had taken a heavy toll of the ships in the East coast convoys during the course of the war, and green wreck buoys were far more common in those parts than the various types of buoy which showed the safe channels through the banks.

Suddenly, a Spitfire flew low over the water towards us from the South-west and circled us. Then it flew low overhead and rocked its wings as it sped back in the direction from which it came. Obviously, it was giving us a signal that we were to follow in the direction of a dinghy or a man in the water, so Andy increased speed and altered course. Back came the Spitfire pilot, repeating the procedure and rocking his wings madly, as if impatient with our inability to make more haste.

Meanwhile, Andy had called down our new course and speed and I was checking our position on the chart. Finding that we were heading dangerously across the sandbanks to starboard, with a number of wrecks dotted about them, I went up to the bridge to warn Andy and get a visible check on the bearing of the buoys in the tideway.

'We must keep well to port of that conical wreck buoy,' I warned, noting that, although our course should in theory be taking us safely past, the wind and tide were exerting an unusually powerful force and likely to carry us too far to starboard. Andy, too saw the danger.

'Alter course South-East,' he ordered, just in time to ensure that we would pass to port of the buoy.

It was the third hour of the tide, which meant that we should have enough depth of water. But that was also the time when the tide was at its strongest, forming powerful races as it was funnelled through the narrow channels between the banks. We seemed to be managing to keep the buoy to starboard, but we were quite close by now and the sea, broken against the banks by a strong wind, was causing us to pitch heavily. We decided to change course again. But the buoy must have been driven out of its correct position, in relation to the wreck, by the force of the sea and the shifting sands. The tide also would have been carrying it to the southernmost limit of its moorings, so that it was no longer far enough to the East of the wreck to ensure our safety. We rose on a particularly high wave and, as we plunged down again into a deep trough, the whole ship shuddered and a mighty thump made our hearts miss a beat. We had hit some part of the wreck! We waited in horror for a crunching of timbers to follow our first contact with whatever was hidden beneath the surface, but a second wave picked us up and lifted us clear. We plunged on past the buoy and hastily took stock of our position.

'Carpenter, sound the bilges!' is the traditional order, which Andy claims was his automatic cry, although we carried no carpenter, despite being an entirely wooden ship. Naturally, however, the engine-room staff started up the pumps and reported that, fortunately, we were not taking in water.

The remainder of the below-decks crew had come tumbling up on deck with a speed which would have done them credit at a call to action stations. They were never entirely at ease down in their mess-deck in the fo'c'stle, when the bows were thumping into an oncoming sea, and threatening to sever it from the rest of the hull. This mighty crack underneath the keel, beneath their feet, now made that seem an even greater probability.

However, we were soon able to establish that we had not suffered sufficient damage to cause anxiety and we set a more prudent course in the general direction taken by the aircraft. Not long afterwards we were even more annoyed to find that the apparent rescue call turned out to be a false alarm.

The following day, we had, of course, to report the incident and draw up a full account of the damage that had been sustained. We went across to the slip at Harwich to have the ship's bottom examined and we found that a large chunk of wood had been gouged out of the sturdy wooden keel. As we had plunged down into the trough of the wave it must have hit a razor sharp piece of projecting metal. Fortunately nothing penetrated the thin double skin of mahogany which formed the hull and the wooden frames were undamaged. We were due for a refit in December, in any case, so shortly afterwards we headed for the Blackwater and the boatyard at Wivenhoe, on the river Colne near Colchester.

For the first time for most of us, since joining the Navy, we enjoyed Christmas leave at home, although London was still a target for the rockets and flying bombs. On my way to Plymouth, I spent a night at my uncle's house in Wandsworth. It was disturbed at regular intervals by the sound of explosions caused by rockets, against which there was no protection, so all I could do was pull the blankets over my head and try to get some sleep. I remember quite clearly looking up into the sky as I made my way in the morning to Waterloo station, to watch a buzz-bomb flying overhead. As long as it kept flying, there was no need to worry, but suddenly people started to run for shelter as its engine cut out. I anxiously watched it fall and explode somewhere in Lambeth. It might be worth noting here that, during the course of the war, people developed a very stoical attitude to air attacks of most kinds. If there was nothing they could do about it, they realised it was pointless to panic and they became much more casual in their response to danger than most people today realise. I took part recently in a community play at the Plymouth Theatre Royal to celebrate the fiftieth anniversary of the Plymouth blitz. I found it impossible to persuade the director that it was unrealistic to assume that all the crowds carried gas masks everywhere they went or spent all night in air raid shelters. It wasn't heroism, simply the fact that we would have had no fun at all, and never survived if we had allowed ourselves to be so terrified the whole of the time. The important thing was to relax and get as much enjoyment as possible out of being alive. In fact, in some ways many people had a lot more fun during the war than in peacetime. That was why the V1 and V2 attacks proved ineffective in damaging public morale.

In early January I returned to find the East coast in the grip of an arctic winter, which had delayed progress on the boat. She was still high and dry on the slip, covered with a thick layer of ice and snow. I was obliged to spend the first night back on the empty boat. It reminded me of my very first night in the Navy, shivering in arctic conditions in a freezing chalet at Skegness. The total lack of facilities made it impossible to live on board so, feeling just a little guilty, when Andy arrived we went into shore quarters in a large country house at Brightlingsea, discovering just how luxuriously some of the people on shore could live, even in wartime. I thought I was dreaming at first, when I woke to find a pretty Wren in my room instead of the accustomed gangling, gloomy Bowler. Unfortunately she had only come to bring me a cup of tea and open the curtains. But the sight of her was luxury enough.

The headquarters of the Naval Officer in Charge of the little Brightlingsea base, who controlled a fleet of two or three motor boats, turned out to be a cosy waterside pub, requisitioned for the duration. He directed operations from the comfort of the saloon bar, complete with pool table, pin-ball machines and no restrictions on opening hours. He also had a primitive kind of fruit machine, which must have given him a useful extra income, for it seemed incapable of producing a jack-pot. As it was also the ward-room, we spent our days there in a permanent atmosphere of gin and 'Passing Clouds'. Time passed very pleasantly between receiving and making the one or two signals a day by which contact was maintained with Nore Command. When at last the thaw set in, and the boat was ready for sea again, we caught the little branch-line train back to Wivenhoe with great reluctance, although in the meantime we had missed all the activity connected with the German offensive in the Ardennes.

I now had a second wavy stripe on my sleeve, having been promoted to Lieutenant on January 1st, on the completion of the regulation two years as a Sub. In fact, all of us were now full lieutenants, except the Number One of 550, who had replaced Mac many months before. Mac had qualified for his second stripe just before we left Immingham, in time to move to a command. Now, with the war in its last phase, there were too many officers for the ships, so we stayed where we were. We had also been joined by the four boats no longer needed at Appledore, to make an eight-boat flotilla, with Lieut Scott as SO.

Andy and I were brought back to harsh reality on the first day of our return to duty. Once again we were sent to a waiting position near Sunk Head Fort and once again, as we made our way through the channels, we were vectored to a ditching a few miles to the South-East. This time there was enough water to get us over the banks and a course clear of wrecks. We were contacted by a Walrus and given a more precise bearing, together with the information that a fighter pilot had been forced to bale out. Presumably, like Foster, it was because of engine failure.

Unlike Foster, however, it seemed that he had had the usual difficulty in making a successful fall into the water, since the Walrus crew next reported that they were circling over a body, floating on the surface.

We carried on, however, at full speed, and soon sighted two Thunderbolts which had joined the Walrus in orbiting a flame float, which had been dropped as a marker. We learnt from the Walrus that the body was right beside the marker, then, a few minutes later, that the body had disappeared, presumably because the flame had burst the poor chap's mae-west, which had been keeping his body afloat. We searched the sea all around the spot, but all we were able to find was an aircraft wheel and a section of fuselage from the fighter aircraft.

Even though Germany was now hard pressed on both fronts, East and West, the war was still exacting its toll.

CHAPTER 19

The End of the E-Boats

One of the most tragic finds by an ASR launch in our part of the sea was made by HSL 2558, one of the RAF launches which co-operated with us at times. This time, however, it was not the result of a ditching.

In the last months of the war, as the allies occupied more and more of Europe, there were fewer calls upon our services for the rescue of ditched airmen, although we continued our patrols as usual. Aircraft in difficulties could make emergency landings in the liberated areas of the Netherlands and did not need to risk the sea-crossing. However, the E-boats based at the Hook of Holland had not given up the fight, and they still maintained their threat to the East coast convoys.

We used to see the anti-E-boat flotillas heading past us every evening, on their way to head off these dangerous attackers. They usually consisted of a frigate from Harwich, accompanied by a group of MTBs and MGBs from *Beehive*. A highly co-ordinated plan of operations had been evolved, making use of the latest advances in radar and VHF communications. Specially equipped Wellington aircraft patrolled overlapping areas of the enemy coastline and reported E-boat movements to ships and to a plot on shore. This enabled the frigate, or sometimes destroyer, supporting and guiding the Coastal force craft, to organise an interception before the enemy could engage a convoy. Other units from Yarmouth and Lowestoft, placed strategically to the North, would be ready to cut off their escape.

On the 6th of April, with the war drawing inexorably towards its close, the E-boats came out to make a last gesture of defiance. Six of them slipped out of Den Helder just before the Wellington arrived to patrol that particular box, and were on their way across the North Sea before they were picked up by a second aircraft 31 miles South-West of Ijmuiden. The conditions were ideal for E-boat operations: there was no moon, no phosphorescence to reveal their presence. The sea was smooth, with only a slight swell, and visibility, to eyes accustomed to night fighting, was good. Luck was on their side, too, because that night there was so much interference from other radio traffic that the Wellington's sighting report was held up for thirty-five minutes, giving them time to get right through to the convoy route without being intercepted.

As the E-boats closed the line of buoys which marked the swept channel through which the convoys passed, the Harwich group, with the destroyer *HMS Haydon*, was still too far to the South to engage them. However, *HMS Cubitt* came down from the North at full speed, guided by direct VHF contact with the shadowing Wellington, and at 0046 picked up the enemy boats on its own radar, as they sped westward into the swept channel. The destroyer opened fire and its captain could see its guns scoring hits on the low, sleek hulls of the enemy. Unable to head further into the shallow waters of the coastal channels, the E-boats' commander did just what the destroyer captain had expected. He turned North, into the trap which had been set for him. For MTBs 781 and 5001 had been left to lie in wait a little further to the North. Now they were ordered to steer West to intercept and they were almost on top of the enemy when they sighted them, heading at right angles across their bows, in line ahead.

MTB 781 immediately aimed at full speed for the nearest E-boat and just missed ramming it by a few feet, passing close astern and raking it with gunfire as it passed through its wake.

Then MTB 5001 also broke through the enemy's line, exchanging fire with the boats to port and starboard. Turning to starboard, in a classical Nelsonian manoeuvre, both MTBs continued to engage the enemy at close range as the E-boats swung round and headed South-East to escape their attackers. Although badly damaged, they returned the fire and a shell from the powerful stern gun of one of them hit 5001 in the engine room and forward tank space. This was a particularly vulnerable spot. Most British boats suffered a vital disadvantage compared with the enemy: they were driven by highly inflammable petrol whereas the Germans had powerful diesels. Their fuel was much less likely to explode. The MTB soon became a mass of fire. Beaten for speed, 781 had to abandon the chase and go to the aid of her blazing companion. Forty minutes later it blew up and sank, with the loss of three ratings killed and wounded.

The E-boats, which had turned again and were now heading at full speed for home, may well have thought that they had escaped further danger, but the Wellington, J/524, was still following their movements. It now brought another patrol group into action. This was one of two units of three MTBs each which, listening to the action reports coming over the VHF, had moved South from its patrol position to intercept, leaving the other unit to protect the northern patrol area. When the three MTBs came within radar range, the crew of the Wellington were able to plot the positions of the two opposing groups and provide ranges and bearings to direct the British boats on to the enemy.

The two forces approached each other at right angles, at high speed, each seeing the other suddenly loom up to port or to starboard in the darkness. It was then a moment for quick decisions and rapid manoeuvres, to ram or avoid being rammed, to turn and bring all guns to bear, or to cut through the line and steer a parallel course with all guns blazing.

In the leading British boat, MTB 494, the Senior Officer, Lieut. Jack May, headed for the first of the E-boats as they approached his bows from right to left. He had just opened fire, preparing to ram, when he himself was rammed amidships by the second in line. Although the boat was badly damaged, his guns' crews continued to fire.

In MTB 493, Lieut. A.D. Foster had just enough time to observe the exchange of fire between the leaders before another wake appeared fine to starboard and the third E-boat was sighted less than fifty yards away. Instinctively, Foster drove at full speed into the port quarter of this boat, then went full astern to pull his boat away and crashed the engines into full speed ahead again. Passing through its wake, he turned to port and pursued it at close quarters, pouring shells and bullets into the stricken enemy. At a range of only twenty-five yards, he observed five six-pounder hits on the E-boat. Then, suddenly, his ship stopped with a crunching shock, as the already damaged bow ploughed into the submerged hull of MTB 494. From now on he found it impossible to go ahead: the ship would go astern only.

MTB 494, though virtually cut in two, had continued firing to the last, and now several men were in the water around the wreck. Lieut. Foster, unable to manoeuvre properly to reach them, had to call to them to swim towards him. After one man had been picked up, a red Very's light was seen coming from an E-boat lying stopped about two hundred yards away. Not knowing whether this was a signal to others to come to the attack, Foster moved astern, clear of the wreck and the survivors, and illuminated the enemy with rocket star-shell, opening fire again upon the enemy craft. The latter, however, did not return his fire and continued sending up red Very lights, so 493 ceased firing.

Meanwhile, MTB 497, commanded by Lieut. Harrington DSO, had, in its turn, headed straight into the rear of the enemy line, opening fire on two E-boats which were crossing its bows. Suddenly, another boat came speeding in on a ramming course and Harrington had to take violent avoiding action, reducing speed and flinging the ship over to port, so as to come on a parallel course. Opening fire at only ten yards' range, 497 scored a hit with the six-pounder and sent a number of shells from the Oerlikon into the E-boat, pursuing it on the port quarter as it drew away. A stoppage in the six-pounder and a failure in the rocket projector prevented further damage to the enemy so, learning over the intercom of the damage to 493 and the presence of an E-boat near to her, Harrington abandoned the chase and returned to the scene of the battle.

The two surviving MTBs exchanged recognition signals, by means of the fighting lights at their mastheads, and 493 illuminated the scene with star-shell, whilst 497 approached the stopped E-boat. As she passed the wreckage of 494, cries of distress were heard and Harrington searched for survivors, picking up three of her crew.

He next approached the E-boat, with an armed boarding party in readiness, and hailed the captain in German, which he could speak fairly fluently.

'Do not abandon ship,' he called.

'I cannot move, come alongside and take off my wounded and crew,' replied the E-boat captain.

By the light of the Aldis projector the German crew could be seen sitting or standing about the upper deck, making no attempt to abandon ship and obviously waiting to be taken off. Some were even smoking.

'I have some seriously wounded. Take us off, we shall sink in seven minutes,' he shouted.

This precise timing rang an alarm bell in Harrington's mind. All our boats had scuttling charges in the bilges, which were primed ready to explode as soon as we set off a fuse by crushing a metal tube at the end of a wire. No doubt the same applied to the E-boats. As soon as his crew were safe, the German Captain intended to scuttle his ship. Harrington was determined to bring the E-boat back to port if at all possible, so he ordered, 'Remain on board. I will take you in tow.'

In spite of the other's protestations, Harrington refused to take anyone on board and insisted on towing. Realising there was no alternative, the German suddenly became helpful and suggested that he should be towed by the stern. Accordingly, a stout hawser was passed from the E-boat to the MTB.

But then 497's Motor Mechanic reported overheating problems on the main engines, which meant that the tow had to be handed over to MTB 775, a member of the other patrol unit, which had now moved South to lend its assistance. In spite of the efforts of this MTB and its partner, MTB 764, the attempt to bring in the E-boat proved unsuccessful and it sank before daybreak.

While all this was going on, lights were seen flashing to the southward, and so 497 went to investigate. Harrington found that these came from groups of German survivors from another E-boat, who were picked up and made prisoners. After a further search of the area, 497 set course for Lowestoft.

There was still a need to attend to 493, which was painfully struggling to make course for home by going astern on both engines. At length, a following swell and overheating engines made it impossible for her to continue unaided. MTB 5020 therefore closed her to take her in tow and managed to bring her into Lowestoft at 1010 in the morning. The engagement with the enemy had taken place around 0200 and the other MTBs had returned to harbour at about 0600. Although their own losses were heavy, two, probably three, E-boats had been sunk and the others damaged by gunfire. It was the last E-boat attack of the war.

E-boat arriving at Felixstowe, May 1945

E-boats alongside dock at Felixstowe

But that was not the end of the story of that night's action. On the following day, a patrolling Catalina flying-boat spotted a number of rafts near the scene of the battle, virtually in the middle of the North Sea, half-way on a direct line between Cromer and Den Helder. It directed HSL 2558 to the spot, where five British and three German life-rafts were found, together with a Q-type dinghy. All were empty of survivors, having been probably those from which 497 had picked up a number of men. The HSL then returned to its patrol position, while the Catalina continued to search the area.

Soon it reported another raft, which this time appeared definitely to contain survivors. When 2558 went to investigate, it found that the raft contained the bodies of a Lieutenant RNVR and three British naval ratings. They were, in fact, Lieutenant Jack May and three of his crew. What had happened to them following the sinking of 494 no one now can tell. Perhaps they had been badly wounded and put in the raft by their comrades soon after the boat was hit. Perhaps they had been too weak to call for help or had even succumbed to their wounds before 497 came back to pick up the few survivors. One can only hope that they did not lie suffering for hours, hoping in vain for rescue. The HSL had the sad task of bringing back the last of 494's dead, which, in addition to Lieutenant May, included the First Lieutenant, the Midshipman and eleven members of the crew. The German prisoners told their captors that, although their ship was cut in two and sinking, the gunners kept up their fire to the last. Only a few weeks after they gave their lives, so heroically, and in some ways so unnecessarily, all the rest of us were celebrating the end of the war in Europe.

The conduct of the demoralised enemy was in sharp contrast. With their boat disabled, they made no attempt to continue the fight. Harrington also reported that the men he picked up from the life-rafts had become very anxious when he was manoeuvring slowly amongst them. They shouted, waved white flags, and made the V-sign and they scrambled aboard with great alacrity as soon as he came alongside. The second group had to be ordered to stay in their raft to help their seriously wounded officer, whom they were prepared to leave to fend for himself.

The E-boats did leave their base once more. On May 12th they sailed unscathed from Den Helder to the British coast. In the afternoon of Sunday the 13th, they appeared off Felixstowe, in line ahead, with white flags at the masthead and their guns pointing skywards. They sailed up the river, turned to starboard past the long wooden pier of Felixstowe harbour and into the dock, to moor alongside the wall among the boats with which they had fought so fiercely for so long. The sides of the dock were crowded. Everyone was there, anxious to see what these prowlers of the sea were really like.

Their officers went ashore to make their formal surrender to the Captain of *Beehive*, whilst we, on 547, carried out our very special task. We had our crew turned out in their number one uniforms. Those not required for handling ropes and fenders were placed at strategic points armed with the sub-machine-guns which throughout the war had remained unused, locked in the arms cabinet. Clem Woodhead was up in the crow's nest, and Boswell was beside me at the port gangway. Our job was to take off the crews and transport them to Shotley, on the other side of the estuary, past Harwich, where they would be temporarily kept under guard. We went smartly alongside and I motioned to the men gathered on the decks to come on board. They filed meekly and glumly along our deck towards the fo'c'sle, where they lined up in a none too orderly bunch. One, as he stepped towards our gangway, was smoking a cigarette, which was not only unseamanlike, but dangerous aft of the funnel, near the fuel vents, so I rapped out my one German phrase, learnt from the notices on the petrol barges:

'Rauchen verboten!'

He leapt in alarm, and his startled eyes fixed on the revolver which I had taken from the holster strapped to my hip – the first time I had handled one since my initial training long before. In a second he had stubbed it out and he scuttled aboard in terror to join his comrades. There were forty-seven all together, crammed in front of the wheelhouse. They stood meekly and silently, with a chilly wind blowing about their ears as we crossed the estuary, a very ordinary, dispirited bunch of men, who seemed to bear no resemblance to the image of a fierce, relentless enemy which most people held in their imagination. We marched them off again at Shotley pier, and turned them over to the Naval training establishment at *HMS Ganges*. Then we went back to moor alongside the E-boats again, on which we had left an armed guard.

We had to maintain a guard on them for the remainder of the night to keep souvenir hunters away. This gave us, however, an opportunity to look them over and compare their living quarters and equipment with ours. They were extremely well designed, with low, sleek lines, which made them a difficult target to hit. The armoured bridge and gun turrets were sunk low into the hull and the torpedo tubes were enclosed, forming an integral part of the hull, like the bow of a submarine. On our boats, guns and torpedo tubes were completely exposed, being simply bolted to the upper deck, whilst the bridge was the most dangerous place to be. When we were in training, we viewed with some apprehension the possibility of being posted to the Dover flotillas, where the life expectancy of a first Lieutenant, stuck in the wheelhouse, was rumoured to be about two weeks! On the after deck they had a powerful Bofors type gun and racks for mine-laying from a low counter. Painted white, with fierce emblems on the side, such as a large black panther, they gave an impression of fearsome efficiency as fighting boats.

Their slim, conventional bilge keels made them excellent sea-boats, whereas our MTBs were flat-bottomed, with hard-chine keels, which made them plane over the water, quite unsuitable for anything but calm weather. They had the edge on our boats for speed, because in their engine-room they had two long rows of gleaming, powerful diesels, which had the added advantage of being less vulnerable to fire. They were also more lightly and more strongly constructed on aluminium alloy frames. Our only comparable diesel boat was the Camper and Nicholson, such as were used on the blockade running to Sweden. There were only a few of these, however, for some inexplicable reason.

However, we were not at all impressed with the very restricted living quarters. They were not only cramped but very dirty. The cupboards were infested with cockroaches, the bilges were full of filth and there was an all-pervading stench of ersatz tobacco and other odours. In our navy, at First Lieutenant's rounds each morning, the slightest sign of dirt or dust would be pounced on. Everything had to be kept spotless and tidy, however small the ship might be.

So, the war with Germany was over. We listened to the news of the final days of the Reich, the capture of Berlin and the death of Hitler. The lights went up again. We celebrated the return of all that we had longed for during the dark days and nights when peace and normality seemed so far away. Our songs had been so charged with sentiment – 'When they sound the last all clear', 'I'm going to get lit up when the lights go up in London', 'We'll meet again' – that there was a certain amount of anti-climax, somehow, with nothing much to do or to worry about any more. My own reaction was dampened to some extent because I had just been jilted by a pretty blonde Wren with whom I had formed a long-standing attachment. I had found out that while I had been at sea over the past month or two she had been two-timing me with one of the officers on the base staff, and I was consequently pretty 'chokka' about it. It was more wounded vanity than a broken heart, however, since I had no intention of getting serious, with the prospect of several years of study ahead of me.

I had to get busy with checking over mess accounts, settling the crew's tobacco and chocolate accounts, doing inventories of all the special clothing, oilskins, rum, food, guns, ammunition, mess-traps, crockery, cutlery, bedding, charts, instruments, everything that was movable in the various lockers throughout the ship and for which the captain was officially

E-boat crews transferring to 547

547 leaving with E-boat crews

responsible. We had to find ways of accounting for anything missing by means of the various forms relating to equipment lost at sea, washed overboard by giant waves or supplied to survivors and not returned after going ashore. They took some very strange things with them. But with the prospect of paying-off looming near, we had to make sure everything was accounted for. The Captain was responsible for anything missing, and Andy recalls having a fierce argument over a piece of equipment which we had never used and with a purpose and name unknown to us. He dug out of a cupboard what he thought was this strange object and offered it to the stores accountant, only to be told it was not the 'ten inch Hankins gorbal cranker', or whatever it was, on his list. In the end he was forced to pay twenty-five pounds for the alleged missing item. He never discovered what in fact it looked like or what its function was supposed to be.

Equally boring was the work we were given to keep us occupied. We loaded up regularly with boxes of out-of-date ammunition of all kinds and dumped it in designated parts of the North Sea. Some of us were used as ferries across to Rotterdam and Antwerp. However, we didn't mind the job of taking groups of Wrens out on trips, to give them a taste of the ocean, from which they had been barred for so many years. I had a letter recently from one of them, recalling the thrill of going to sea on 547!

Andy was able to take his wife and seven-year-old son for a trip on the boat which they had only been able to visit occasionally in the dock. Young Stuart was able, to his great delight, to fire off some of the surplus ammunition from the Lewis guns, and found himself deaf for four days as a result. Everyone enjoyed the last opportunity to blast off with tracer, rockets, machine-guns, flares, hand grenades and depth-charges, which were now surplus to requirements.

Within a few weeks the whole scene had been transformed. The base had been rapidly run down. Officers and men had disappeared to barracks or to ships destined for the Far East. Strings of abandoned small craft appeared, moored to lines of buoys in the Harwich roads and up the estuary of the Orwell. We had a grand paying-off party at the end of June, which ended with a few more members joining the Dunkers' Club before the list was finally closed. Then the flotilla was sent back with skeleton crews to Dartmouth, to be laid up at the line of buoys where we had waited for D-day. It was goodbye to all the fun we had enjoyed, all the friends we had made, all our favourite haunts in the little seaside town. The Pavilion on the sea-front, with its big dance floor, crowded night after night with laughing servicemen and women; the Felix, the luxury hotel at the eastern end of the promenade, where the MGB and MTB officers sometimes let loose their tensions in wild parties; the little dock basin, crammed with small craft, at the end of the dingy road through the wasteland to the west of the town. Only Hichens and his comrades, in the cemetery on the hill, were left behind to bear silent witness to the part Beehive had played in keeping up the offensive throughout the war in Europe.

For Andy it was a sad moment as he looked back at his 'yacht' being stripped of its fittings and lined up in Dartmouth with the dozens of other boats whose duties were over. What would be the next move, he wondered – Japan?

After a spell of leave back at Felixstowe, he received a signal appointing him to take command of HMS Wastwater, which was a converted Antarctic whaler, completing repairs at Gibraltar. Her existing Captain was an Australian who was wanted back at home. However, before he could order his tropical kit and read up the Admiralty Fleet Orders about service in the Far East, fresh instructions came through. The Magistrates' Court at Stratford, London, where he had been the clerk of No. 2 Court, was now so overloaded with work that an application was made for his temporary release. This was granted, becoming permanent almost immediately with the ending of the war with Japan. He went on to become a qualified Solicitor and to spend periods as Clerk to the Justices at South Shields and finally the

County of Berkshire. After his retirement in 1972, he and his wife, Jay, enjoyed a Round the World trip of eight months. Now, at eighty, they spend their winters in their villa in Spain, calling in on my wife and myself as they come and go. With his grizzled beard and ruddy cheeks, he still looks the same cheery old salt as he did years ago.

I was sent to *HMS Cabbala*, a shore establishment near Manchester, to join a number of other redundant Coastal Force types and Wrens with educational qualifications on a course to prepare us for EVT. In other words we were due to be employed as instructors on a grand scheme aimed at providing 'Educational and Vocational Training' for people heading for civvy street. We were to help them obtain qualifications through a 'Forces Prelim' exam, roughly the equivalent of a School Certificate. We were given a course of about three weeks in teaching methods and the organisation of an educational centre, which was remarkably practical and well organised. Of course, this might have been expected, considering the effort that the Navy had had to put into devising efficient training methods to produce all the navigators, engineers, radar, signals and other specialists that the war had required. The films and film-strips they produced for teaching navigation and ship handling, for example, were well in advance of anything previously used in education, and the simulated torpedo attack and gunnery trainers were great fun. At the torpedo school in Brighton, you really felt that you were on the bridge of an MTB in the early light of dawn, aiming at the distant shapes of German ships as they moved across the horizon. For the new task there was no expense spared. There were stores full of text-books, books on all subjects from which libraries could be created, ample supplies of typewriters for commercial courses, and a comprehensive range of books and pamphlets offering careers guidance. Long before the end was in sight, someone had been planning and preparing with great thoroughness for the peace.

I was fortunate enough to be posted to a small camp, in the countryside just outside Plymouth, to help to found an EVT centre offering engineering, art, business and language courses. It consisted of a group of grimy Nissen huts in a dank and gloomy wood. However, I was able to live at home and drive there each day in my ancient, 1931 model, 7 hp Jowett saloon purchased earlier in the war for use on leave. The only snag about this antiquated but remarkably capacious vehicle was that it was a poor starter and a slow runner, with a 25 mile maximum range before the engine gave up the ghost and demanded an hour or so's rest. It was excellent for short hauls and on occasions it carried as many as eight RNVR and Wren passengers to dances and parties. I was not always able, however, to get it started in time to reach the camp before morning divisions. I remember making a catastrophic beginning on my first day, by roaring into the centre of the camp in the middle of prayers, scattering the neatly drawn up ranks right and left, while a red-faced, bull-necked, apoplectic First Lieutenant bore down on me, quivering with rage. He was an ancient ex-ranker, with little time for young RNVR upstarts and I had well and truly blotted my copybook with him. It was perhaps just as well that only a few months remained before the Japanese surrendered and the demob started. Having still to complete my university degree course, I was given priority for demob, and so November saw me collecting the generous hand-out of a tight-fitting suit, raincoat and trilby with which we were all returned to civvy street. Instead of taking my demob leave, I went straight back to London to become a student once again, adjusting to a very different world.

It was good to renew acquaintance with old friends, as they trickled back from service in all parts of the world, but in some ways the change was unsettling. We tended to be almost too conscientious in working to make up for lost time; we fretted at the slowness and inadequacy of many of the tutors, set in their ways and lacking the imagination to cope with mature young men, accustomed to an active existence. At the same time, we were a generation apart from the youngsters just out of school. The food, too, with rationing still in force, was inadequate after service rations. We tended to be impatient and critical and eager to be out in the real world again. I took my degree in 1947, did a year's teacher training and embarked on a career in Education.

In the summer of 1946, I made a pilgrimage back to Dartmouth and saw the old boats lying there still, lonely and deserted in mid-stream. It was, I think, in 1951 that I found a group of ex-RMLs in use again in Torbay. They were being used as ferries, carrying holiday-makers across from Torquay to Brixham. The camouflage paint and their numbers had been covered over and they were individually unrecognisable. The sick bay and after accommodation had been converted to take the trippers. I foolishly took a trip to Brixham and back, banned from the bridge, a mere nobody, passively seated on the upper deck. It was a mistake. Whether this was 547 or not, I had no sense of belonging. She was a mute hulk and I was an ordinary civilian. The war was over for both of us and our ways had parted for good.

Thirty years later, I returned to Felixstowe dock, with my wife, to meet a large tanker on which our daughter was returning with her Merchant Navy husband from America. The giant port installations made it totally unrecognisable, and in the town I could recognise none of the old haunts, where we had had so much fun. We spent a dismal evening in a dull hotel which seemed to have replaced the old Wrens' quarters and drove home at the earliest opportunity.

Nothing remains of those days which played such a significant part in our lives. Never again will the skies be full of great bomber fleets, gleaming silver against the hazy blue, or dark and menacing as they gather in the deepening dusk. Never again will the majestic procession of great battleships sail from Scapa, with the lean, grey shapes of the escorting destroyers spread wide over a foam-flecked sea. Never again the sudden clutch of fear at the heart, as the wail of sirens rises to a crescendo and the throb of enemy engines precedes the whistle of falling bombs. The face of war has changed.

But still the memory of those days persists, and is preserved by the numerous old comrades associations whose newsletters reflect the enormous impact made on our generation by the experiences we went through. The community play in which I took part, in 1991, at the Plymouth Theatre Royal, revived almost too vividly the memory of what the city suffered in the blitz, fifty years before. I found myself, together with many others, deeply affected by simple, even banal reminders of life in those days. The sentimental songs stirred long-vanished emotions, the sounds of sirens and falling bombs and the girls in uniform brought it all back, the tension, the longing for peace and the relief when at last it was all over.

I can still imagine myself back on the bridge on a cold, dark night, watching the slow rise and fall of the bow over an ink-black sea, as the evening star seems to guide us on our way. I can see the rising moon spreading a golden path towards us across the velvet water, and causing the spray from the bow wave to throw up a cascade of sparkling fluorescence along both sides of the boat. In winter storms, we would ship it green right over the bridge, and our eyes and ears would be caked with salt. Coming back to land on a calm morning, the shallow waters would reflect the pale greens and greys of the sky, streaked with the faint rose of dawn, and the low line of the coast would appear hazily in the mist, a scene which I longed to have the skill to paint. There was a peculiar magic about that life at sea.

Looking back, I do not regret the experience of danger through so much of the war, but I feel relieved that I was able to spend so much of it in a service which was concerned with saving life rather than destroying it. I was never a belligerent type and have grown even less so over the years. I think often of the many schoolfriends whose lives were cut short by the war. As many as forty names on my old school's roll of honour commemorate boys I knew. A number of them flew with the RAF during those years when casualties were so high. I think with regret of all that they had to sacrifice but I am glad that there are many others still alive thanks at least in part to 547 and the 69th RML Flotilla.

CHAPTER 20

The ASR Organisation

As these accounts of rescue operations show, there was a gradual and considerable improvement in rescue services during the course of the war, brought about by the need to sustain morale in the heavily increased air offensive and by the technical innovations of the Americans. Our own suggestions based upon experience made a contribution, too.

At the start, there was only a small RAF Marine Service, backed up by small commandeered motor boats such as Andy was sent to command after he entered the Navy. Their purpose was largely to cover ditchings near the coast, mainly by aircraft on training flights. But the Battle of Britain, the gradually increasing raids on Germany and occupied France and the Battle of the Western Approaches, where Sunderlands, Whitleys and Wellingtons carried out dangerous sorties against U-boats, made it necessary to provide long-distance rescue services.

By 1942 the Navy was contributing a number of RML flotillas to supplement the HSLs of the RAF. They were based in harbours all round the coast, such as Falmouth, Newhaven, Yarmouth, Lowestoft, Immingham, Stornoway and Appledore in North Devon. Basically the same Fairmile MLs as were used for convoy escort and had made an important contribution to the raid on St Nazaire, they were larger than the HSLs (110ft compared with 64ft). With on-board living accommodation and greater fuel capacity, they could stay longer at sea. Their conventional bilge keel made them better able to endure rough weather so, although they were much slower, they were much better suited for long distance searches than the HSLs with their hard chine, power boat hulls. Their sick bay, too, gave them better facilities for attending to injured survivors.

They usually operated in tandem with the RAF launches and both branches of the service were operated by a controller, normally a RAF officer, attached to each of the Naval Command Headquarters at Nore, Western Approaches etc. He would receive notice of air operations planned for each day and organise suitable ASR cover, sending the boats to pre-arranged patrol positions near to the flight paths of the aircraft. As reports came in of mayday distress calls, of ditchings or sightings of dinghies, the controller would arrange for air searches and order the nearest boats to the position given. He would amend this as further information was received and finally decide whether to hold the boats at a waiting position or to recall them to base if the search proved unsuccessful. Since signals had to be relayed to and from the boats and aircraft separately, via their local bases, there was considerable delay in communications. This was a great disadvantage, because the relative positions of boats and dinghies could have changed in the meantime. When a boat eventually received its orders and set out towards the position which it had been given, the dinghy would have already been carried some distance away from its original position on the chart by wind, tide and local currents. The search needed to be based, at its start, on their relative positions in the water, rather than on the chart. Even then they would each be affected differently by the weather and the sea as the search developed. Also, although search aircraft could cover a vastly greater area of sea, they too were affected by wind and weather conditions. So a successful search involved making judgements based on a number of factors. With few navigational aids – no log to measure speed, no echo sounder, no radio beacons – the important requirements were experience of wind, weather and sea and careful attention to the greatest possible accuracy in navigation.

There was no guarantee that the reported position of a dinghy was correct in the first place, since the aircraft could have flown on for some distance after sending out a mayday call, or a reported sighting might not have been pin-pointed with total accuracy. This could make the task of the boats, with their slow speed and limited visibility, more difficult still, since they then had a greatly increased area to cover.

Nowadays, with satellite navigation and automatic distress signals, with computers, helicopters and long-distance communications, we seem to live in a different world. But the kind of experience we acquired still seems to be needed. Recently, after an intensive search for a small boat off the Welsh coast had been abandoned, the exhausted occupants were fortunately driven ashore on Lundy Island. This was just one case, amongst others, when the searchers had misjudged the power of the wind.

Communication and co-ordination between boats and search aircraft was absolutely vital. They were supposed to communicate on the 500kc international frequency for distress calls. Unfortunately in the early years Halifax and Stirling aircraft from squadrons placed on stand-by were often used. Geoffrey Jones in his book, *Night Flight* gives accounts of often frustrating searches in Halifaxes. The difficulty was that the crews were not fully briefed or experienced and did not know how to communicate with the boats. They were unaware that they should contact us on 500kcs and continue to transmit continuously on this frequency, whilst orbiting a dinghy, so that we could home on them by means of our direction-finding aerial. This was what hampered us so severely in the early part of 1943.

In the earlier stages, when the boats had reached the position where the dinghy was most likely to be, allowing for the effects of wind and tide since the time of ditching or sighting, it was necessary to decide on the best form of search to adopt. If there was little wind and a calm sea, a simple box search would be carried out. The lead boat would plot a course East, then North, West, South and East again in the shape of an ever increasing square. The second boat would be positioned on the starboard beam, at twice the estimated visibility distance, depending on the state of the sea. This enabled them to cover a strip of water four times the visibility distance, so that the fourth leg of the square was increased each time by this amount. With the tidal currents now affecting both boats and dinghy equally, there would be no allowance for tide, except in working out the true position over land. Downwind legs might be made longer if the wind was likely to be carrying the dinghy more rapidly before it, out of the box.

If a strong wind was blowing, a key search might be decided upon, covering a wide area of sea in successive strips, downwind. Chapter 11 illustrates the success of adjusting the search plan in the light of wind strength, and the rescue of Flying-Officer Foster again shows how intuitive adjustment to wind strength and direction could find a dinghy which even the search aircraft had lost.

By 1943, however, things began to improve. Great strides were being made in persuading aircrews to take sensible steps to increase their chances of being rescued if they were forced to ditch. They were encouraged to carry out ditching and dinghy drill and make sure that their dinghies were fully provisioned and properly maintained. Efforts were made to convince them that if they carried out their drill effectively there was every chance that they would be rescued. Our interchanges of visits played a part in this. The RAF's Directorate-General of Aircraft Safety became responsible for researching the best means of providing rapid assistance to ditched aircrews. The records show that case histories were studied in detail and all kinds of ideas were considered.

One special provision was the mooring of small, permanent floating refuges at intervals some miles off the East Coast. If an airman could manage to reach one of these, there was shelter, food and radio communication with the shore. There were times when these proved useful, although naturally it was unlikely that many aircraft would be able to ditch near enough to benefit from them.

The biggest advance was the establishment, in mid-1943, of special ASR squadrons, consisting at first of Hudsons, such as we visited at Bircham Newton, in Norfolk. Wellingtons were also used and the larger version of this aircraft, the Warwick, specially fitted for Air-Sea Rescue, took over in 1944. The Americans, very conscious of the need to ensure the safety of their airmen flying in huge numbers across the North Sea by day, provided the stubby, round-nosed Thunderbolt fighters as low-level search aircraft and provided everyone, boats included, with VHF crystal sets working on fixed frequencies. With a flick of a button, we could talk directly to both the Thunderbolts and the Warwick which, flying above the bomber formations, would shepherd them home, co-ordinating any rescue operations which were needed. A simple vector was all that was needed to speed a boat on its way, a vast improvement on the cumbersome earlier system.

The other great advance was the introduction of the airborne lifeboat, designed to be streamlined into the underpart of the fuselage, first of the Hudsons and later of the Warwicks of Coastal Command. Their designer was the famous Uffa Fox, and they were intended at first to enable airmen who had ditched close to the enemy shore – off Heligoland, for example – to sail or motor away from the coast and then signal to the rescue services on the small radio with which they were equipped. They were 22ft long, rather narrow, and fully equipped with a mast, Bermuda rig sail, dagger plate and rudder, all of which had to be shipped in the right order after boarding. They had two 1½ hp Britannia engines and, in lockers in the bottom of the boat, stores, warm down suits and cans of petrol – later marked 'GAS' for the benefit of the Americans!

They were winched up tightly to the under body of the aircraft, over the bomb bays. Two metal stanchions held the boat tightly to the fuselage and the gunwhales were padded so as to keep out the wind. They were released by the bomb release. The pilots weren't very happy about the drop procedure, as they had to fly at almost stalling speed and only about 600ft above the sea, so that they did not have much room to recover if any problem arose. Nevertheless, they saved hundreds of lives in the North Sea, right out to the coast of Denmark.

Although not the first vessel to rescue a crew from a lifeboat, RML 547 was the first to both rescue a crew from one and bring back the lifeboat. The experts were anxious to see how the boat had performed in the actual rescue, and Andy was able to point out several factors. This particular crew had gone through a very testing time, fighting very heavy seas in a full gale (see Chapter 7) and they certainly owed their lives to the lifeboat, in spite of the problems that they had to overcome.

There were many stories of the difficulties that arose. Mention has already been made of the American crew who were unable to start the engines because they could not find any 'Gas'. Another crew started the engines while the parachute lines were still about and fouled the propeller. The parachutes were supposed to be released automatically as the boat touched the water, by means of an hydraulic switch, but this did not always work and, on one occasion, the boat was carried away at a merry speed, with the parachutes still attached, acting as a spinnaker. During tests, three were dropped by Lancasters but, owing to a failure to fix the holding strop properly, they went straight down into the sea and sank.

By the end of the war in Europe, they had become 30 feet long and had an Austin 7 engine in a rubber bag and a propeller which came out through a tube. There was a hatch in the deck to free the prop if it jammed. They were double-skinned mahogany, with canvas between the skins, and they had rock-elm timbers. The decking was marine ply and they were kept afloat by buoyancy chambers filled with carbon dioxide gas from bottles operated by a tilt switch or an immersion switch. As the boat landed on the sea, other immersion switches caused rockets to send out a floating drogue, which acted as a sea anchor, and to fire buoyant lines in all directions, so that the survivors could grab one and pull themselves to the boat.

When released from the aircraft, they were adjusted to land on the water at a 17 to 20 degree angle, so as to glide in and not break their backs.

One of the problems after the war was that personnel were demobbed so rapidly that hardly anyone was left who had any experience about the inspection, safety and equipment. The Safety Equipment base at Thorney Island had been manned mainly by Australians, who, when the war ended, wanted to get back home. By then, helicopters were coming into service and the next thing was to design a harness for lifting people straight out of the water on a wire.

The RAF was still, however, considering what improvements could be made to the lifeboat, and an interesting suggestion was that, in view of the difficulty that distressed airmen had in reaching the boat and climbing aboard, and then sailing it, it would be better if the lifeboat could be landed with a coxswain aboard. He would be able to reach the airmen, bring them aboard, and then sail the boat to a rendez-vous point or harbour. The problem was, however, that it was becoming apparent that the shape of the boat that was developing did not necessarily agree with the shape of the underside of the aeroplane, and also it was thought to be rather risky for the coxswain to have to go down in the boat. It was then suggested that the lifeboat could become a glider, towed behind the rescue plane and launched over the site, so that the coxswain could pilot it down and then, if necessary, jettison the wings and proceed as a boat. Further, in places such as the far North, where a rescue might have to be carried out on the ice sheet, the glider would be able to land and then, when all was ready, be snatched up again by the rescue aircraft and towed back to safety. The RAF would have had to invent a rank of 'Pilot Coxswain', but the continuing development of the helicopter service finally made the lifeboat redundant.

After the war, quite a number of the lifeboats were bought up by Ian Proctor, an Olympic Yachtsman, and when Andy visited him at that time, he was in the process of converting them to racing boats to fill a need for private craft, which had become scarce due to the war.

Mention should also be made of the Sunderland and Catalina flying-boats of Coastal Command and the Walruses of the Fleet Air Arm. The latter, operating from their base at Martlesham, were, as has been seen in Chapter 15, constantly active over the southern part of the North Sea, landing to rescue airmen when conditions were suitable or directing rescue craft to dinghies. They had the disadvantage that they had little room in the fuselage for survivors and they were easily damaged if they landed in anything but a very calm sea. Quite a number of crews had to be rescued along with the men they had gone down to save.

There are many accounts of the heroism of Sunderland, and later Catalina crews, going to the rescue of airmen in distress in the wider reaches of Western Approaches. Bombers returning from St Nazaire and Brest, or reconnaissance planes searching for U-boats in the Bay of Biscay might be shot down by fighters or the submarines they were trying to depth-charge. It was at great risk to themselves that the flying-boats descended into the heavy Atlantic swell and there was constant danger from the long range Focke-Wulf 200 Kondors or from shore-based Junkers and Heinkels. In Chaz Bowyer's *Men of Coastal Command* there are some tragic accounts of rescuers themselves becoming casualties, giving their own lives in the attempt to save others, or enduring days of agony, far from land, awaiting rescue by Naval vessels.

One such rescue involved Flight-Lieutenant Allan Triggs and the crew of his Wellington, forced by engine failure to ditch 180 miles South of Land's End. They had managed to get off a mayday call giving their position and were found next day by a Whitley with Beaufighter escort. However, the Sunderland which came to rescue them that evening broke up on landing in the growing swell and only one survivor, F/O J. Watson, managed to reach a dinghy previously dropped by the Whitley. Late next day, a Whitley which had signalled that help was on the way was pounced on by a group of German Arados and shot down with no survivors: the radio traffic must have alerted the enemy to the presence of the dinghy. Two more weary days passed before more Beaufighters and Hudsons appeared and dropped supply containers, but these were followed by four Focke-Wulf fighters. Although these German pilots merely waved to the men in the dinghy, they were soon seen chasing a Beaufighter, which fortunately shook them off.

On the sixth day, by which time they had managed to reach and give help to F/O Watson, three Hudsons and two Beaufighters set up an air umbrella over them, keeping at bay three Arado 196s, which were circling on the northern horizon, while RML 180 and three other RMLs came at full speed towards them. As RML 180 was taking the seven airmen on board, a German motor launch, escorted by Fw 190s, appeared and one of the fighters began to make an attacking run on the Naval boats, while the Hudsons took refuge in the clouds. Pounced on by a Beaufighter, the Fw turned away trailing smoke.

The danger was not over yet, however, for, as the four RMLs took station and started for home, they were attacked by the remaining Fw 190s and had to defend themselves fiercely as cannon shells whipped into the water all round them. Driven off by the launches and the Beaufighters, the Fw 190s left the scene, only to be replaced by a Kondor and a Ju 88, which was intercepted by a Beaufighter as it started a dive towards the boats. For a further three hours, the Kondor continued to shadow the little flotilla, ultimately giving up as the boats got nearer to Newlyn, where the survivors were landed.

This was an excellent example of the persistence and sacrifice of the men of Coastal Command in coming to the rescue, regardless of the proximity of the enemy. It demonstrated also the long distance role of the RMLs and the co-operation between the Naval and Coastal Command services.

This co-operation developed progressively during 1943 and 1944, resulting in ever-increasing numbers of airmen being rescued from the sea.

Statistics show how important the ASR cover was both to morale and to the maintenance of trained manpower. In 1942, of approximately 3,000 airmen ditching in the sea, 1016 were rescued to be returned, in most cases, to active service. This number rose to 1684 in 1943 and was hugely increased in 1944. By the end of October, 1944, the total number of aircrew rescued in home waters had risen to 5,390. This figure did not include any non-flying personnel.

The map on page ii shows the large number of incidents reported in the period from April to September, 1944, not including the many more resulting from operations Overlord and Market Garden. It can be seen that, in the Nore area, a high proportion were successful, i.e., resulted in at least one life being saved. Incidents classified as unsuccessful included those where only bodies or empty dinghies were found, those relating to aircraft simply reported as missing or overdue, those regarded as not practicable because of weather conditions or because they occurred too close to the enemy coast, and those for which there was no evidence that there was ever any survivor to rescue. As our experience showed, there was almost no hope for bomber crews baling out individually at sea, a heavy casualty rate amongst fighter pilots, and no guarantee that a ditching in bad weather would be successful. It would seem, therefore, that by late 1944 the organisation could at last claim to be functioning with a high degree of efficiency.

Appendix 1

Rescues of USAAF personnel by 69th RML Flotilla

Date	Aircraft	Position	Survivors	Boat
21/5/43	Fortress B.17.F. 229666	100 miles E. of Grimsby	10	RML 553
28/7/43	Fortress 544 Sq 384 Gp	Danish fishing boat 54.38N 02.32E	10	RMLs 547, 550
11/7/44	Liberator 704 Sq 446 Gp	51.45N 02.31E	1 + 2 from Walrus	RML 547
11/7/44	Liberator L 2201 732 Sq 453 Gp	51.51N 02.15E	9	RML 547
20/7/44	Liberator 862 Sq 493 Gp	078 Felixstowe 27m	9 + 1 body	RMLs 520, 512
21/7/44	Fortress 305 Gp	37 m E of Clacton	1 + 1 body	RML 520
31/7/44	Fortress 332 Sq 94 Gp	25m E Aldeburgh	9 + Walrus crew	RML 520, HSL 2722
9/9/44	Mustang 334 Sq 4 Gp	122° Felixstowe 55m	1 + Walrus crew	RML 550
12/9/44	Lightning	40m E of Aldeburgh	Walrus crew only	RML 520
13/9/44	Lightning 364 Sq 357 Gp	106° Felixstowe 41m	1 + Walrus crew	RML 550
18/9/44	Dakota 306 TCS Sq 442 Gp	090° Felixstowe 68m	4	RML 547
18/9/44	Dakota	092° Felixstowe 53m	4	RML 550
5/10/44	Mustang 505 Sq	128° Orfordness 11m	pilot picked up by trawler, Walrus crew by RML 547	
9/10/44	Mustang 334 Sq 4 Gp	092° Felixstowe 51m	1	RML 547
14/12/44	Bomber	N Galloper buoy	7	RML 550
11/1/45	Fighter	51.43N 01.31E	wreckage only	RML 547

RML 547 Incidents relating to RAF Personnel, 1943–1945

Date	Aircraft	Position	Survivors
3/8/43	Mitchell, 226 Sq.	55.08N 04.17E	3 of crew with RML 553
4/9/43	Lancaster, 106 Sq.	54.23N 03.07E	5 + 1 dead, with RML 550
22/1/44	Halifax LKJ, 51Sq.	54.19N, 01.01E	4 + 1 dead, with RML 520
11/7/44	Walrus 278 Sq.	105° Felixstowe 45m	2 crew + aircraft
17/9/44	Glider No 462 D Sq.	100° Felixstowe 76m	5 survivors
5/10/44	Walrus 278 Sq.	090° Felixstowe 18m	2 crew
23/9/44	Lancaster (on outward flight, crashed in flames)	51.41N 01.21E	2 bodies

Other rescues by boats of Q69. RML Flotilla:

Out of Immingham up to June 1943:

RML 553 2 Beaufighter crew

RMLs 547 and 550   5 from fishing boat

RMLs 520 and 553   3 Wellington crew

RMLs 520 and 553   1 from Halifax

Out of Felixstowe:

6/10/44   3 of Heinkel crew RML 550

On 18/10/45, the *East Anglian Times* reported on the closure of the Felixstowe base, *HMS Beehive*, stating that the Air-Sea Rescue flotilla carried out 589 patrols and rescued 121 airmen from the North Sea between July 11th, 1944 and June 20th, 1945

Appendix 2

RML 547 'Dunkers' Club'
List of members

Thomas D. Estes 1st Lt.	28 July 1943 Fortress, 544 Sqn 384 Gp USAAF
David H. Davis 1st Lt.	do
T/Sgt W.J. O'Donnell	do
S/Sgt Fred. S. Wagner	do
S/Sgt George Ursta	do
Lt James M. Minitt AC	do
S/Sgt J.M. Self	do
S/Sgt Burton G. McDuffie	do
T/Sgt David L. Cochran	do
1st Lt. John J. der Bois	do
Sgt Lecomber RAF	3 August 1943 Mitchell 226 Sqn RAF
A.P. Eyton-Jones P/O RAF	do
Sgt D.W. Bishop RAF	do
S/L Howroyd + 4 members of crew	4 September 1943 Lancaster JA893 106 Sqn RAF
Sgt Melville	22 January 1944 Halifax LKJ 51 Sqn RAF
Sgt Godfrey	do
Sgt Chapps	do
Sgt A.F. Mansfield	do
T/Sgt Jack Millar	11 July 1944 Liberator 704 Sqn 446 Gp USAAF
R.C. Whittaker W/O	11 July 1944 Walrus 278 Sqn R.A.F.
Paul J. Ray F/O	do
Arthur L. Nueller 2nd Lt AC	11 July 1944 Liberator L2201 732 Sqn 453 Gp USAAF
Ambrose L. Prouhet 2nd Lt. AC	do
T/Sgt William E. Griffiths	do
T/Sgt Charles Sams	do
Sgt William D. Cornstock	do
2nd Lt. J.T. Gunnell	do
S/Sgt D.O. McCormick	do
S/Sgt S. Leibner	do
2nd Lt. J.R. Barnett	do
Eugene N. Lancer (or Larner) 6463022 1st Paras	17 September 1944 Glider 462 D Sqn
H. Rogers 2061532 1st Paras	do
CQMS W. Cook DCM 4543011 1st Paras	do
Sgt G. Tapping 7594973 Glider Pilot Rgt	do
S/Sgt K.D. Beard 6291974 Glider Pilot Rgt	do
Flt/O Logan C. Atterbury	18 September 1944 Dakota 306 TCS Sqn 442 Gp
S/Sgt Nicholas J. Carone	do
Lt. William J. McCormick Jr	do
S/Sgt Jimmy Powell	do
W/O F.J. Bedford FAA	5 October 1944 Walrus 278 Sqn FAA
L/A B. Westbrook FAA	do
F/O K.E. Foster USAAF	9 October 1944 Mustang 334 Sqn 4th Fighter Gp

Assorted members of US Army Transportation Corps and Royal Navy

Appendix 3

NOTICE BOARD ISSUE OF
NORE GENERAL ORDERS

321. Air Sea Rescue
The following letter of appreciation has been received from the Officer Commanding H.Q. VIII Bomber Command, United States Army:–

I wish to express my gratitude and that of every member of this command, to the officers and men of your Air Sea Rescue organisation. Due to their efficiency and devotion to duty, the Air Sea rescue recovered 78 crew members of this command on 25th and 26th July.

This rescue by your organisation of crew members who go down because of enemy action has definitely increased the morale of my units. They have obtained confidence and surety that everything possible is being done and will be done to help them after their battles. These rescued men will fight again against Germany.

JACK C. TOVEY
Admiral

BEEHIVE, 26 ASR MCU FELIXSTOWE

Copies to Capt, Secy. H.S.Ls. Q69 26 ASR

From C. in C. Nore 241001A

To Midge, Beehive, 24 ASR MCU Gorleston, 26 ASR MCU Felixstowe INFO FOICS Harwich, Yarmouth, AOC 16 GROUP.

Restricted BT.

I congratulate all the RMLs and HSLs that took part in Operation MARKET on their excellent work over a number of days involving long hours sometimes under difficult weather conditions.

Great credit is also due to Base Maintenance staffs whose good work kept so many boats in running order during this most important operation

Awards published in the *London Gazette*, June 14th, 1945:

Lt. S.G. Sheppard R.N.V.R.   M.B.E.
Lt. T.D. Andrews R.N.V.R.   M.I.D.
Lt. E.K. Smith R.N.V.R.   M.I.D.
Lt. D.A.K. Tratner R.N.V.R.   M.I.D.

Copy to Commanding Officer, R.M.L. 547

No. 106 Squadron,
Royal Air Force,
Syerston,
Notts.
11th September, 1943

REH/DO

Sir,

I have the honour to submit the following report on an episode which involved Naval Forces under your command, and I desire to tender my thanks and appreciation, both on behalf of myself and of the survivors of the rescued crew, for the prompt assistance, consideration, and generous treatment shown to them by the Officers and men of the rescuing forces.

One of my Lancaster crews was detailed to attack Berlin on the night of September 3/4th. They were attacked by an enemy night-fighter, and one of the crew killed and another seriously wounded. Due to loss of petrol, the aircraft was forced to 'ditch' in the North Sea, approximately 200 miles from our coast. The crew boarded the dinghy, and after six hours were located by Air Sea Rescue Hudsons. Shortly afterwards, an airborne lifeboat was dropped, into which they transferred themselves.

They were not long aboard this before they were again located, this time by a Naval Rescue Launch, and they were taken aboard, given treatment where necessary, a good, sound meal, and put to bed.

The survivors are most enthusiastic and appreciative of the manner in which they were treated, and of the kindness shown to them by the crew of the Rescue Launch, and of the staff who looked after them when they were landed at Immingham.

I would be most grateful if you would communicate the contents of this letter to all concerned.

I am, Sir,
Your obedient servant,
(Sgd) R.E. Baxter,
Wing Commander Commanding
No. 106 Squadron, R.A.F.

The Flag Officer i/c,
Humber Area, Royal Navy

(The crew was unfortunately shot down, and all but one were killed, only a few weeks later. See Chapter 8)